CHRIST
THE
HEALER

CHRIST THE HEALER

F. F. BOSWORTH

FLEMING H. REVELL COMPANY
OLD TAPPAN, NEW JERSEY

Library of Congress Cataloging in Publication Data

Bosworth, Fred Francis, 1877-
    Christ, the healer.

    Reprint of the 8th ed., with a new introd.
    1. Faith-cure. I. Title.
BT732.5.B67 1974   252   73-17492
ISBN 0-8007-0647-1

CONTENTS

— FOREWORD —

These sermons were first published in response to urgent requests from ministers and others in the cities of the United States and Canada where Bosworth revival campaigns had been conducted. They were prepared under great pressure and weariness from continuous revivals. Since each chapter was originally a sermon, certain foundation truths were repeated in various ways in order to lay a ground work for deeper truths. It was intended, through such repetition, that the understanding of the reader would become so saturated as to drive out certain erroneous teachings imbedded by faithless and impotent traditionalism.

My father made no pretense as to literary style, possessing only a limited education, but through a God-given gift of simple presentation, he stated these deep and logical arguments. This is why this book has become the greatest classic on the subject of Divine Healing and a textbook in church Bible classes, Bible schools, and seminars.

Realizing that most of his ministry had been given to those living in America; F. F. Bosworth, at the age of 75, went to Africa, determined to spend the rest of his life sharing these marvelous truths with those in foreign lands who had been neglected. It would surprise the world if they could read the continuous stream of wonderful testimonies that have come from around the world. Dad received more than 225,000 letters from radio listeners and friends, most of whom he never saw.

The truths discussed in this book, together with "the prayer of faith," have brought healing within the grasp of many thousands of sufferers who could not have recovered without the direct action of the Holy Spirit. To God be all the glory.

While we rejoice in these miracles, we remember that they are only external manifestations of a thousand times greater and more precious miracle which has transpired within the sacred chamber of the inner man. The inner cause is so much more precious than the outward effect. Physical results from prayer are like figures in a bank book which show that you have gold deposited in the bank. The gold is more valuable than the figures.

R. V. BOSWORTH

AUTHOR'S PREFACE

When in the year 1924 we wrote the messages for the first edition of this book, little did we dream that the truths presented were to bless such vast numbers in so many parts of the world. The results, down through the years, have been a demonstration of the truth of the inspired declaration that God "is able to do exceeding abundantly above all we ask or think" (Eph. 3:20).

During the forty-four years which have followed, six more large editions have been printed and read by thousands of ministers and laymen who have written to us telling how they have been enlightened and blessed, soul and body, through reading and re-reading these messages.

In this book we have tried to use the vocabulary common people understand, and a continual stream of testimonies comes to us from those soundly converted and miraculously healed through their own faith which came to them while reading and meditating on the truths of the Bible which we have tried to make plain.

We have proved thousands of times and are continuing to prove, that by the simple presentation of enough of the written Word of God to the minds and hearts of the incurably afflicted, they can be brought to the same state of certainty and assurance concerning the healing of their body as to the healing of their soul.

We are therefore increasingly thrilled over the privilege of planting the "incorruptible seed" — the Word of God — in the hearts of those for whom Jesus died. O what a glorious fact that we have each been "bought with a price" to be the Lord's Garden in which His "imperishable seed" — the Word — are to be continually "planted," "watered" and cultivated, so that they can produce their present and eternal wonders.

In the "seed" there are possibilities beyond the power of the human mind to conceive, just as in a little seed there is a potential tree a million times bigger than the seed. All of God's wonderful works are potentially in the seed. By keeping God's garden planted, as the farmer does his fields, a child of God can accomplish things a thousand times greater than men of the highest human talents can accomplish by fulfilling His promises.

We have found that those who have tuned in the broadcasts of the National Radio Revival, most of whom we have never seen, by reading the healing and other literature we have published, get a much broader understanding than those who hear only an occasional message in our public meetings. Because they can be re-read and studied, we have the proof that our messages in printed form produce better results in the souls and bodies of those for whom we pray, than in some who attend our meetings and desire to be prayed for before they hear enough of the Word of God to produce faith.

This book is sent out with the earnest prayer that many thousands more may learn to appropriate the many blessings promised in the Bible. "We desire that every one of you ... be followers of them who through faith and steadfastness inherit the promises" (Heb. 6:11, 12).

F. F. BOSWORTH

INTRODUCTION

Little did I realize when I published the first popular paper-back edition of this book what a surge of new interest would be generated. When the dust of skepticism, kicked up by the mercenary methods of a decade of "faith healers" had finally settled, there was a deep hunger in the hearts of many sincere Christians for a sane and scriptural presentation of irrefutable Bible truth.

Many men of God have been aware that the Reformation has never been completed; that God seems to be systematically working toward a return to New Testament faith and simplicity so as to eternally silence man's excuse of ignorance of God's message. Fundamental Christianity has suffered great damage through the efforts of some theologians to excuse their own spiritual impotence through relegating everything supernatural into an imaginary transition period of dispensational truth which cannot be scripturally proven. It can only be substantiated through their own interpretation of isolated passages, and is perpetrated through blind traditionalism not unlike that which Christ faced. Yet, deep within the hearts of sincere men there is a longing to rescue the Book of Acts from becoming nothing more than an historical record and to put it back in its proper place as a pattern for the modern church whereby God can continue to confirm His Word and give proof of the Resurrection of His Son in this day of universal unbelief.

When the first simple truths concerning God's attitude toward sickness and human suffering came to my father as a result of intensive study of Scripture, it was like a bright light in a traditional darkness. Not only did God illuminate Scripture, but He confirmed His Word through Dad's personal ministry, healing those beyond the help of medical science, and producing in their lives a depth and holiness of living that could not be attributed to Satan or to man. I'm sure my father did not realize that the truth received was fifty years ahead of its time, and only after it had been proven through his life and ministry could it be used as a major contribution in God's reformation process of returning supernatural power to His church.

Medical science has made great strides in its effort to alleviate human suffering, and yet the accelerated pace of our modern society continues to take its toll on the bodies of men, producing sickness beyond man's ability to help. The demands for sufficient doctors, hospitals, beds, and cures grow with increasing pressure, and many new drugs and medicine are creating new problems. The population explosion has caused problems of poverty, malnutrition, and epidemic disease that can only intensify the message that man needs a Healer God. How the Father nature of God must long for man to return to the security and simple faith of pure fellowship with Him, taking His Word as fact that can be fully trusted!

It is within the context of human need that the greatest message of this book shines forth as a beacon in a faithless world. The church basically has only one message: that in all things, our Heavenly Father can be trusted to honor His Word. Beyond just the message of Divine Healing, this book clearly presents the principles of faith in a way whereby every Christian can discover and possess—through the benefits of Calvary —all that Adam lost. It is to hungry, needy men everywhere that we present this new edition of *Christ the Healer*.

R. V. BOSWORTH
1973

CHRIST THE HEALER

1

To Those Needing Healing

Before anyone can have a *steadfast* faith for the healing of their body they must be rid of all uncertainty concerning God's will in the matter. Appropriating faith cannot go beyond one's knowledge of the revealed will of God. Before attempting to exercise faith for healing, one needs to know what the Scriptures plainly teach, that it is just as much God's will to heal the body as it is to heal the soul. The sermons in this book point out and explain those portions of Scripture which will forever settle this point for you. It is only by knowing that God promises what you are seeking that all uncertainty can be removed and a steadfast faith is made possible. His promises are each a revelation of what God is eager to do for us. Until we know what God's will is, there is nothing to base our faith on.

It is important that the mind of those seeking healing be "renewed" so as to be brought into harmony with the mind of God as revealed in the Bible and pointed out in the following pages. Faith for the appropriation of God's promised blessings is the result of knowing and acting on God's Word (Rom. 10:17). The right mental attitude, or the "renewed mind" (Rom. 12:2), makes steadfast faith possible to all.

We are constantly receiving testimonies from those who, though prayed for repeatedly without success, were afterwards wonderfully healed while reading this book. Many also have been happily converted while reading these instructions.

It would surprise the world if they could read the continuous stream of wonderful testimonies coming to us from all over the country. We have received during the past few years more than 225,000 letters from our radio listeners and their friends, most of whom we have never seen.

The truths discussed in this book together with "the prayer of faith" have brought healing within the grasp of many thousands of sufferers who could not have recovered without the direct action of the Holy Spirit. To God be all the glory.

While we rejoice in these miracles, we remember that they are only external manifestations of a thousand times greater and more precious miracle which has transpired within the sacred chamber of the inner soul. The inner *cause* is so much more precious than the outward *effect*. External results from prayer are like figures in a bank book which show that you have gold deposited in the bank. The gold is more valuable than the figures.

"The Word Is the Seed"

Jesus said, "The Word is the seed." It is the seed of the Divine life. Until the person seeking healing is *sure* from God's Word that it is God's will to heal *him,* he is trying to reap a harvest where there is no seed planted. It would be impossible for a farmer to have faith for a harvest before he was *sure* the seed had been planted.

It is not God's will that there shall be a harvest without the planting of the seed — without His will being known and acted upon. Jesus said, "*Ye* shall *know* the *truth,* and the *truth* shall make you free." *Freedom from sickness comes from knowing the truth.* God does nothing without His Word. "He sent His Word and *it* healed them" are the

words of the Holy Spirit (Psa. 107:20 Fenton's translation).
"All His work is done in faithfulness" to His promises.

For each sick person to *know* that it is God's will to heal
him, is the "seed" which is to be planted in his mind and
heart. And it is not *planted* until it is known and received
and trusted. No sinner can become a Christian before *he*
knows that it is God's will to save *him.* It is the Word of
God planted and watered and steadfastly trusted, which heals
both soul and body. The "seed" must *remain* planted and be
kept watered before it can produce its harvest.

For one to say, "I believe the Lord is *able* to heal me"
before he knows from God's Word that He is *willing* to heal
him, is like a farmer saying, "I believe God is able to give
me a harvest, without any seed being planted and watered."
God can't save the soul of a man before the man himself
knows God's will in the matter, because salvation is by
faith — that is, by trusting the *known* will of God. Being
healed is being *saved* in a *physical* sense.

Praying for healing with the faith destroying words, "if
it be Thy will" is not *planting* the "seed"; it is destroying
the seed. "The prayer of faith" which heals the sick is to
follow (not preceed) the planting of the "seed" (the Word)
upon which alone faith is based.

It is the *gospel* which the Holy Spirit says, "is the power of
God unto salvation," in all its phases, both physical and
spiritual. And *all* the gospel is for "Every creature" and for
"all nations." The gospel does not leave a man in uncertainty
praying with an "if it be Thy will"; it tells him what God's
will *is.* The Holy Spirit's words, "Himself bare our sicknesses"
(Matt. 8:17), are just as truly a part of the gospel as His
words, "Who his own self bare our *sins* in His own body
on the tree" (1 Peter 2:24).

Neither the spiritual nor the physical phase of the gospel
is to be applied by prayer alone. Seed is powerless until it
is planted. Many, instead of saying, "pray for me" should first
say, "teach me God's Word, so that I can intelligently cooperate for my recovery." We must know what the benefits of Calvary are before we can appropriate them by faith. David specifies: "Who *forgiveth* all thine iniquities, Who *healeth* all thy
diseases."

After being sufficiently enlightened, our attitude toward
sickness should be the same as our attitude toward sin. Our
purpose to have our *body* healed should be as definite as
our purpose to have our *soul* healed. We should not ignore
any part of the gospel. Our Substitute bore both our sins
and our sicknesses that we might be delivered from them.
Christ's bearing of our sins and sicknesses is surely a valid
reason for trusting Him *now* for deliverance from both.
When, in prayer, we definitely commit to God the forgiveness
of our *sins,* we are to believe, on the authority of His Word,
that our prayer is heard. We are to do the same when praying
for healing.

After being sufficiently enlightened by the promises of
God, then, by simply believing that our prayer is heard,
before we have yet experienced the answer, as Jesus commanded in Mark 11:24, and following this with the observ-
ance of Hebrews 10:35, 36, we can *always* bring to pass the
fulfillment of any Divine promise. It is God's will for every
Christian to successfully practice Hebrews 6:11, 12.

Between the time we definitely commit to God the healing
of our body, and the completion of our healing, we can, and
should, learn one of the most valuable lessons of our Christian life. And that lesson is, how to observe Hebrews 10:35,
36. Only Divine promises can make our faith steadfast. After

Jonah had prayed for mercy, he did not cast away his confidence because there was yet no visible proof that his prayer was answered. No, he held fast his confidence and added to it, in advance, the sacrifice of thanksgiving (Jonah 2:9). In Hebrews 13:15 the Holy Spirit commands us all to do this "continually."

God's promises work their wonders while we see and act on *eternal* realities (on His promises, His faithfulness, etc.) and refuse to be affected by *temporal* things to the contrary. God always fulfills His promises when He can get the right cooperation. He always accepts us and undertakes for us when we observe Mark 11:24 and Hebrews 10:35, 36. "With long life will I satisfy him" is God's promise to be appropriated by all (Psa. 91:16).

Comprehensive Instructions

In the 4th chapter of Proverbs, from the 20th to the 22nd verses, we have most comprehensive instructions as to how to receive healing:

"Attend to My Words; incline thine ear unto My sayings. Let them not depart from thine eyes; keep them in the midst of thine heart. For they are life unto those that find them, and health to all their flesh."

The Word of God cannot be health to either soul or body before it is heard, received, and attended to. Notice here that the Words of God are life only to those that "find" them. If you want to receive life and healing from God, take time to find the words of Scripture which promise these results.

When God's Word becomes health to all your flesh, your cancer will be gone, your tumor will be gone, your goiter will be gone. We have seen the Word when received and acted upon produce these results thousands of times. The flesh of thousands today is not healthy flesh because they have failed to "find" and "attend" to that part of God's Word which produces healing. This is the divine method of receiving the blessings which God has provided for us. Many have failed to receive healing simply because they have not followed this method.

God says that when we do as we are told in the Scripture, His Words are made "health to all our flesh." It matters not what particular kind of unhealthy flesh — whether cancer, goiter, tumor, etc., God says, "Health to all their flesh." Whose flesh? Those who "Find" and "attend to the Words of God on the subject." This is exactly the same way that the Word of God becomes health to the soul.

Cannot Look Two Ways at Once

In this comprehensive passage, God tells us exactly how to "attend" to His Words. He says, "Let them not depart from thine eyes, keep them in the midst of thine heart." Instead of having your eyes on your symptoms and being occupied with them, let not God's Words "depart from thine eyes;" that is, look at them continually and, like Abraham, wax strong in faith by looking at the promises of God and at nothing else. As the only way seed can do its work is by being kept in the ground, so the only way that God's "imperishable seed" can "effectually work in us" is by its being kept "in the midst of our hearts." This does not mean occasionally, but continuously. The reason why many have failed is because they have not done this.

Must Do As Farmers Do

When we attend unto God's Words by not letting them depart from before our eyes and by keeping them in the midst of our hearts, the seed is in "good ground," the kind of ground in which, Jesus says, "it bringeth forth fruit," and where Paul says, "it effectually worketh." When the farmer gets his seed into the ground, he does not dig it up every day to see how it is doing, but says, "I am glad that is settled" and believes the seed has begun its work. Why not have the same faith in the "imperishable seed" — Christ's Words which He says are "spirit and life," and believe that they are already doing their work, without waiting to see. If the farmer, without any definite promise, can have faith in nature why can't the Christian have faith in the God of Nature.

The Psalmist said, "Thy Word hath quickened me." Paul tells us that it is the *Word* which effectually worketh in them that believe. Every Word of God is "spirit and life" and will work in us when we receive and "attend" to it. When we receive and obey the Word of God, we can say with Paul, "The power of God worketh in me mightily." Thus the *Word* of God becomes the *Power* of God. It is "spirit and life." If a field in which the seed has been sown could talk to us, it would say, "The seed worketh in me mightily."

Three Essential Things

This passage in Proverbs shows us the Method of obtaining results from the promises in God's Word:

1. There must be *the attentive ear.* "Incline thine ear unto my sayings."

2. There must be *the steadfast look.* "Let them not depart from thine eyes."

3. There must be *the enshrining heart.* "Keep them in the midst of thine heart."

When your eyes are upon your symptoms and your mind is occupied with them more than with God's Word you have in the ground the wrong kind of seed for the harvest that you desire. You have in the ground seeds of doubt. You are trying to raise one kind of a crop from another kind of seed. It is impossible to sow tares and reap wheat. Your symptoms may point you to death, but God's Word points you to life, and you cannot look in these opposite directions at the same time.

Which Kind of Seed Have You?

Which kind of seed have you in the ground? "Let not God's Word depart from thine eyes; keep it in the midst of thine heart." That is, look steadfastly and continuously and only at the evidence God gives for your faith. God says to all incurables, "every one that looketh shall live." The word "looketh" is in the continuous present tense. It does not mean a mere glance, but it means, "Let His Words not depart from thine eyes; keep them in the midst of thine heart."

The motives that call for our attention are exceedingly powerful. It is our Heavenly Father Who speaks. All Heaven is behind His Words. The things which are spoken are of quickening and invigorating virtue. They are life to such as find them, and health not only to the soul, but to the body; not to a particular part of it, but to "all their flesh."

A medicine effectual to the cure of a single member of the body might make the inventor wealthy. Here is a medicine for all the flesh — from your head to your feet. Here is a Physician of infinite ability — "Who healeth all·thy diseases."

"The Evidence of Things Not Seen"

After you have planted your seed, you believe it is growing before you see it grow. This is faith which is "the evidence of things not seen." In Christ, we have perfect evidence for faith. Any man or woman can get rid of their doubts by looking steadfastly and only at the evidence which God has given for our faith. Seeing only what God says, will produce and increase faith. This will make it easier to believe than to doubt; for the evidences for faith are so much stronger than those for doubting. Don't doubt your *faith,* doubt your *doubts* for they are unreliable.

O, what a means of blessing is the look of faith to Christ! There is Life, light, liberty, love, joy, guidance, wisdom, understanding, perfect health — in fact everything, in a steadfast look at the Crucified One. No one ever looks in vain to the Great Physician.

Every one that looked at the brazen serpent — the type of Christ — lived. "And their faces were not ashamed," says the Psalmist. They were all, humanly speaking, incurable, but they were both forgiven and healed by looking. He who trusts Christ has no need to be ashamed of his confidence. Time and eternity will both justify his reliance.

This book will show those needing healing just what part of the Word of God they are to receive and "attend" to. Some have been miraculously healed while reading the next sermon in this book.

2

Did Jesus Redeem Us From Our Diseases When He Atoned For Our Sins?

(NOTE—If you, Reader, have been taught to regard sickness as a "thorn in the flesh" which must remain, we would urge you to read the sermon on "Paul's Thorn" before you read any other sermon in this book. Otherwise you will likely miss the force of the scriptural arguments presented in other parts of the book.)

Before answering the above question from the Word of God, I invite your attention to a few facts taught in the Scriptures which bear on this subject.

The Scriptures declare, in Romans 5:12, that "By one man sin entered the world, and *death by sin*." Here it is plainly stated that death entered the world by sin. Therefore it is clear that disease, which is incipient death, entered into the world *by sin*. Now, since disease entered by sin, its true remedy *must* be found in the redemption of Christ. Since the oppression of the devil (Acts 10:38), what power, when nature fails, can remove it but the power of the Son of God? As soon as disease has advanced beyond the power of nature to recover us, it will result in death in every case unless removed by the power of God. This all honest physicians will admit, for they claim only the power to assist nature, not to heal. In this event, anything that would hinder the power of God thus supplementing nature would make recovery impossible. Accordingly, James says, "Confess your faults one to another . . .

14

that ye may be healed" meaning that otherwise ye cannot be healed.

When disease has advanced beyond the power of nature, neither nature, nor the physician, nor even prayer, can save the sufferer until he confesses his sins, unless God, for some sovereign purpose of His own, removes the disease. Since disease is a part of the curse, its true remedy must be the cross, for who can remove the curse but God, and how can God *justly* do it except by substitution? The Bible teaches, as one writer puts it, that disease is the physical penalty of iniquity, but that Christ has borne in His body all our physical liabilities on account of sin, and that therefore our bodies are released judicially from disease. Through Christ's redemption we may all have, as a part of the "earnest of our inheritance" the "life also of Jesus . . . made manifest in our mortal flesh," to supplement nature until our work is finished. In the same way that we may receive the "first-fruits" of our spiritual salvation, we can receive the "first-fruits" of our physical salvation.

Now, to the question,

Did Jesus Redeem Us from Our Diseases When He Atoned for our Sins?

If, as some teach, healing is not in the Atonement, why were types of the Atonement given in connection with bodily healing throughout the Old Testament? In the 12th chapter of Exodus, why were the Israelites required to eat the flesh of the passover lamb for physical strength, unless we can receive physical life, or strength, from Christ, who, Paul says, is "our Passover, sacrificed for us?" 765 years after the institution of the passover, we read in II Chronicles, 30th chapter, 20th verse, that, "The Lord hearkened to Hezekiah, and healed the people" when they kept the passover. Accordingly, Paul, in I Corinthians 11:30, speaks of the failure of the Corinthians to rightly "estimate the body" (Weymouth's translation) of "Christ our Passover" as the reason why many among them were "weak and sickly . . . "

The Lord's Supper is more than an ordinance, because we may partake of Christ while we are partaking of the emblems of His death and the benefits thereof. In Christ there is both bodily and spiritual life, and surely there is no better time for availing ourselves of the privilege of having the "life also of Jesus . . . made manifest in our mortal flesh" (II Cor. 4:11).

Healing Taught in Old Testament Types

Again, in Leviticus 14:18, we read of the priest making atonement for the cleansing of the leper. Why an antonement for the leper's healing if healing for us is not in the Atonement of Christ? The types in Leviticus, 14th and 15th chapters, show us that it was invariably through atonement that sickness was healed. This, to our mind, is a complete answer to the question we are discussing, should we go no further, because all of these typical atonements point to, and prefigure Calvary.

Again, Jesus tells us, in Luke 4:19, that He was anointed "to preach the acceptable year of the Lord," referring to the Old Testament year of Jubilee. This shows us that the year of Jubilee is strikingly typical of gospel blessings, for here He, Himself, applies the year of Jubilee to the Gospel era.

Leviticus 25:9 shows us that no blessing of the year of Jubilee was to be announced by the sounding of the trumpet until the Day of Atonement. On this day a bullock was slain as a sin-offering, and the mercy seat sprinkled with blood. No mercy was offered until the blood of the atone-

ment sprinkled the mercy seat, because it would be a judgment seat if not sprinkled with blood. This teaches us that
no mercy or blessing of the Gospel is offered to us irrespective of Christ's Atonement.

Recovery of All Lost in the Fall

Through the Fall we lost everything. Jesus recovered all
through His Atonement. It was on the Day of Atonement
that God said, "Ye shall return every man to his possession."
The order in the year of Jubilee is, *first* the atonement, *then*
the sounding of the trumpet of the Jubilee, with the glad
tidings "ye shall return every man to his possession." So,
now, the order is the same; *first,* Calvary, *then* the Gospel
trumpet that He "bare our sins" and "bare our sicknesses,"
etc., to be sounded "to every creature;" showing us that we
may return "every man to his possession."

God's seven redemptive names, one of which is Jehovah-
Rapha, "I am the Lord that healeth thee," shows us what
lost possessions "every man" may return to during our dispensation. The two outstanding possessions to be restored
during the Gospel era are health for soul and body; therefore, forgiveness and healing were offered universally wherever Christ preached "the acceptable year of the Lord," in
order that the "inner" and "outer" man might be whole
and ready for the service of God, "thoroughly furnished unto
every good work," so they could finish their course.

Some of the Fundamentalists who attack the Christian
Scientists for believing we can be saved irrespective of Calvary make exactly the same blunder when they say they
believe in healing but that it is offered irrespective of Calvary. It is to me, as well as to them, a mystery how anyone
can say that the blood of Christ was just as efficacious flowing
in His veins as it was shed, in the face of every bleeding

sacrifice of the Old Testament to the contrary and the statement "without the shedding of blood there is no remission of
sins." Adopt a bloodless religion and you have but a religion
of ideas, and nothing but a human thrill, because "joy
unspeakable and full of glory" can never be known except
by those who have been saved through the blood of Christ.
It is just as great a mystery to me how these Fundamentalists
can say that healing is bestowed without reference to Christ's
death. The salvation of any part of man without sacrifice is
unknown in Scripture.

If bodily healing is offered and is to be preached irrespective of Calvary, why was it that no blessing of the year of
Jubilee was to be announced by the sounding of the trumpet
until the Day of Atonement? Paul tells us that it is *"in Him"*
that all the promises of God are yea and amen; which is
another way of saying that all the promises of God, including
His promise to heal, owe their existence and power exclu-
sively to the redeeming work of Christ.

Healing Not Deferred Until the Millennium

Some ministers are trying to relegate bodily healing to the
Millennial Day, but Jesus said *"this day"* (not the Millennial
Day) is this scripture fulfilled in your ears." It was in the
Church (not the millennium) that God set (established)
"teachers, miracles, gifts of healing," etc. None *in the Church*
will need healing during the millennium, because they will
receive glorified bodies before the millennium, when they are
"caught up to meet the Lord in the air," when this mortal
puts on immortality. If we are going to relegate healing to
the millennium, we shall have to do so with the "teachers,"
etc., that God set in the Church, with the "gifts of healing."
To say that healing is only for the millennium is synonymous

with saying that we are now in the millennium, because God is healing many thousands in this day.

God's all-inclusive promise is to pour His Spirit upon all flesh during the "acceptable year of the Lord," which is the dispensation of the Holy Spirit. He comes as Christ's executive, to execute for us all the blessings of redemption — to bring to us "the earnest" or "firstfruits" of our spiritual and physical inheritance, until the last enemy, which is death, is destroyed, thus admitting us to our full inheritance.

Faith Comes by Hearing

The reason why many of the sick in our day have not returned to their physical possessions is that they have not heard the trumpet sound on this line. "Faith cometh by hearing," and they have not heard; because many ministers had their Gospel trumpet put out of order while in the theological seminary. They remind me of a man whom I knew who played a trombone in a brass band. At the beginning of a rehearsal the boys put a small spike into the mouth-piece of his horn, so that, when he blew, his breath went against the head of the spike, making it impossible for him to produce much sound out of the horn, but he went through the whole rehearsal without discovering what was wrong. Some preachers, like this man, think they are blowing their Gospel trumpet all right, and have not discovered that there is not half as much coming out of it as there ought to be. They are not, like Paul, declaring "the whole counsel of God."

As here in Leviticus the types show that healing was invariably through atonement, so Matthew 8:17 definitely states that Christ healed all diseases on the ground of the Atonement. The Atonement was His reason for making no exceptions while healing the sick. "He . . . healed all that were sick, that it might be fulfilled which was spoken by Esaias, the prophet, saying: Himself took our infirmities and bare our sicknesses." Since it is our sicknesses He bore, His Atonement embracing us all, it would require the healing of all to fulfil this prophecy. Jesus is still healing all who come to Him with living faith, "that it might be fulfilled . . ."

Since in the darker age of the types they all had the privilege of being healed, surely in this "better" dispensation, with its "better" Covenant and "better" promises, God has not withdrawn this Old Testament mercy. If so, we are robbed that much by the coming and Atonement of Christ.

In Numbers 16:46-50, after 14,700 had died of the plague, Aaron, as priest, in his mediatorial office, stood for the people between the dead and the living and made an atonement for the removal of the plague — the healing of the body. So Christ, our Mediator, by His Atonement, redeemed us from the "plague" of sin and sickness.

The Type of the Brazen Serpent

Again, in Numbers 21:9, we read of the Israelites all healed by looking at the brazen serpent which was lifted up as a type of the Atonement. If healing was not to be in the Atonement, why were these dying Israelites required to look at the *type* of the Atonement for bodily healing? Since both healing and forgiveness came through the *type* of the Atonement, why not to us through Christ, the Antitype? As their curse was removed by the lifting up of the brazen serpent, so Paul tells us that ours is removed by the lifting up of Christ (Galatians 3:13).

Again, in Job 33:24, 25, we read: "I have found a ransom (margin, atonement), his flesh shall be fresher than a child's; he shall return to the days of his youth." Here, we see Job's flesh was healed through an atonement. Why not ours?

Again, David opens the 103d Psalm by calling upon his soul to bless the Lord and to "forget not all His benefits," and then he specifies, "Who forgiveth all thine iniquities, who healeth all thy diseases." How does God forgive sin? Of course, through the Atonement of Christ. He heals disease in the same way, because the Atonement of Jesus Christ is the only ground for any benefit to fallen man. How can God save any part of man except through the Atonement?

In I Corinthians 10:11, Paul tells us "All these things happen unto them for ensamples (margin, as types); and they are written for our admonition upon whom the ends of the world (ages) are come." In Galatians 3:7, 16, 29, the Holy Spirit shows us clearly that these things are for Gentiles as well as for Israel. "Know ye, therefore, that they which are of faith the same are the children of Abraham . . . now to Abraham and his seed were the promises made . . . and if ye (Gentlies) be Christ's ye are Abraham's seed, and heirs according to the promise." "Therefore ye are no more strangers and foreigners, but fellow-citizens with the saints and with the household of God."

The Rev. Daniel Bryant, in his book "Christ Among Our Sick," says, "The Church then learned what the Church needs, it seems, to learn again; namely, that there is no difference to the compassionate Christ between a sick Gentile and a sick Israelite."

The Seven Redemptive Names of Jehovah

To me, another unanswerable argument that healing is in the Atonement is to be found in the seven redemptive names of Jehovah. On pages 6 and 7 of the Scofield Bible, Mr. Scofield, in his foot-note on the redemptive names, says that the name "Jehovah is distinctly the *redemptive* name of diety," and means "the Self-existent One Who reveals Himself." These seven redemptive names, he says, "point to a continuous and increasing self-revelation." He then says, "In His redemptive relation to man, Jehovah has seven compound names which reveal Him as meeting every need of man for his lost state to the end."

Since it is His *redemptive* relation to us that these names reveal, they *must* each point to Calvary where we were redeemed, and the blessing that each name reveals must be provided by the Atonement. This the Scriptures clearly teach.

The following are the seven redemptive names:

JEHOVAH-SHAMMAH—"The Lord is there," or present, revealing to us the *redemptive* privilege of enjoying His presence, Who says, "Lo, I am with you always." That this blessing is provided by the Atonement is proven by the fact that we are "made nigh by the *blood* of Christ."

JEHOVAH-SHALOM—The Lord our Peace, reveals to us the *redemptive* privilege of having His Peace. Accordingly Jesus says, "My peace I give unto thee." This blessing is in the Atonement, because "the chastisement of our peace was upon Him" when He "made peace by the blood of His cross."

JEHOVAH-RA-AH is translated "The Lord is my Shepherd." He became our Shepherd by giving "His life for the sheep," therefore this privilege is a *redemptive* privilege, purchased by the Atonement.

JEHOVAH-JIREH, means "the Lord will provide" an offering, and Christ was the Offering provided for our complete redemption.

JEHOVAH-NISSI, means "the Lord is our Banner," or "Victor,'" or "Captain." It was when, *by the cross*, Christ triumphed over principalities and powers that He provided for us, through the Atonement, the *redemptive* privilege of saying, "thanks be unto God which giveth us the *victory* through our Lord, Jesus Christ."

JEHOVAH-TSIDKENU, is translated "the Lord our Righteousness." He becomes our righteousness by bearing our sins on the cross; therefore our *redemptive* privilege of receiving "the gift of righteousness" is an Atonement blessing.

The Lord Our Physician

JEHOVAH-RAPHA, is translated "I am the Lord thy Physician," or "I am the Lord that healeth thee." This name is given to reveal to us our *redemptive* privilege of being healed. This privilege is purchased by the Atonement, for Isaiah, in the Redemptive Chapter, declares, "Surely He hath borne our sicknesses and carried our pains." For the sake of the argument, I have reserved this name for the last. The fact is, that the very first Covenant God gave after the passage of the Red Sea, which was so distinctively typical of our redemption, was the covenant of healing, and it was at this time that God revealed Himself as our Physician, by the first *redemptive* and covenant name, Jehovah-Rapha, "I am the Lord that healeth thee." This is not only a promise, it is "a statute and an ordinance." And so, corresponding to this ancient ordinance, we have, in the command of James 5:14, a positive ordinance of healing in Christ's name as sacred and binding upon every church today as the ordinances of the Lord's Supper and of Christian Baptism. Since Jehovah-Rapha is one of His redemptive names, sealing the covenant of healing, Christ, during His exaltation, could no more abandon His office of Healer than that revealed by each of His other six redemptive names. Have any of the blessings which His redemptive names reveal been withdrawn from this "better" dispensation?

Having considered some of the types which teach healing, let us now consider the Antitype—the Atonement itself, as it is described in the great Redemptive Chapter, the 53d of Isaiah, the greatest chapter of the greatest of the prophets, in which is fully stated the doctrine of Atonement. Since the types of the Old Testament taught healing, it is certainly unwarranted and illogical to place the Antitype on lower ground.

He Carried Our Pains

Before quoting from this chapter, may I state that the Hebrew words *choli* and *makob* have been incorrectly translated "griefs" and "sorrows." All who have taken the time to examine the original text have found, what is everywhere acknowledged, that these two words mean, respectively, "sicknesses" and "pains," everywhere else throughout the Old Testament. This word, *choli* is interpreted "disease" and "sickness" in Deut. 7:15; 28:61; I Kings 17:17; II Kings 1:2; 8:8; II Chron. 16:12; 21:15; and other texts. The word *makob* is rendered "pain" in Job 14:22; 33:19, etc. Therefore the prophet is saying, in this 4th verse, "Surely He hath borne our sicknesses and carried our pains." The reader is referred to any standard Commentary for additional testimony on this point; but there is no better commentary than Matthew 8: 16, 17.

An Inspired Commentary

That Isaiah 53:4 cannot refer to disease of the soul, and that neither of the words translated "sickness" and "pain" have any reference to spiritual matters but to bodily sickness alone, is proven by Matthew 8:16, 17 — " . . . and He cast out the spirits with His word, and healed all that were sick; that it might be fulfilled which was spoken by Esaias, the Prophet, saying, Himself took our infirmities, and bare our sicknesses." This is an inspired commentary on this 4th verse of Isaiah 53, plainly declaring that the prophet refers to bodily ailments, and therefore the word "sickness," *choli*, must be read literally in Isaiah. The same Holy Spirit who inspired this verse quotes it in Matthew as the explanation of the universal application by Christ of His power to heal the body. To take any other view is equal to accusing the Holy Spirit of making a mistake in quoting His own prediction.

I will here quote the learned translator, Dr. Young, in his version of the Bible:

3. He is despised, and left of men,
    A man of pains (Heb., *Makob*), and acquainted with sickness (*choli*),
    And as one hiding the face from us,
    He is despised and we esteemed him not.

4. Surely our sicknesses (*choli*) he hath borne,
    And our pains (*makob*) he hath carried them,
    And we—we have esteemed him plagued,
    Smitten of God and afflicted.

5. And he is pierced for our transgressions,
    Bruised for our iniquities,
    The chastisement of our peace is on him,
    And by his bruise there is healing to us.

6. All of us like sheep have wandered,
    Each to his own way we have turned,
    And Jehovah hath caused to meet on him
    The punishment of us all.

10. And Jehovah hath delighted to bruise him;
    He hath made him sick (*choli*);
    If his soul doth make an offering for guilt,
    He seeth seed—he prolongeth days.

12. . . . With transgressors he was numbered,
    And he the sin of many hath borne,
    And for transgressors he intercedeth.

Dr. Isaac Leeser, the able translator of the Hebrew English Bible, renders these verses as follows:

3. "He was despised and shunned of men:
A man of pains and acquainted with disease.

4. "But only our diseases did he bear himself,
And our pains he carried.

5. "And through his bruises was healing granted to us.

10. "But the Lord was pleased to crush him through disease."

Rotherham's translation of the 10th verse is "He hath laid on Him sickness."

From You and Me to Calvary

In the 4th verse, the word "borne" (*nasa*) means to *lift up*, to *bear away*, to *convey*, or to *remove to a distance*. It is a Levitical word, and is applied to the scapegoat, that bare away the sins of the people. "The goat shall bear (*nasa*) upon him all their iniquities *unto* a land not inhabited; and he shall let go the goat in the wilderness" (Lev. 16:22). So Jesus bore my sins and sicknesses away "without the camp" to the cross. Sin and sickness have passed from me to Calvary —salvation and health have passed from Calvary to me.

Again, in this 4th verse of the Redemption Chapter the Hebrew verbs for "borne" and "carried" (*nasa* and *sabal*) are both the same as are used in the 11th and 12th verses for the *substitutionary* bearing of sin, "He shall bear (carry) their iniquities," and "He shall bear the sin of many." Both words signify to assume as a heavy burden, and denote actual substitution, and a complete removal of the thing borne. When Jesus bore our sins, our sicknesses and our pains, He bore them away, or removed them. Both these words mean *substitution*, one bearing another's load.

On this point, permit me to quote from "JESUS OUR HEALER," a splendid tract written by the Rev. W. C. Stevens, published and sold by the Biola Book Store of the Torrey Bible

Institute, Los Angeles, California. He says, "This prophecy presents healing as an integral part of the vicarious Atonement . . . Now, whatever be the sense of these two Hebrew verbs (*nasa* and *sabal*), the same sense must be applied in both cases, namely, of sin-bearing and sickness-bearing. To pervert the sense in one case would give liberty to pervert it in the other. And that the sense of the verbs as relating to sin, not only here in this prophecy, but everywhere else in the Old Testament, is strictly vicarious and expiatory, no evangelical student disputes. This prophecy, therefore, gives the same substitutionary and expiatory character to Christ's connection with sickness that is everywhere given to His assumption of our sins.

An Inspired Translation

We are accordingly shut up by the Spirit to the redemptive sense of Christ's bearing of sickness. This interpretation is fully sustained by Prof. Delitzsch's exposition of Isaiah 53:4. Freely but faithfully does the Gospel of Matthew translate this text, "Himself took our infirmities and bare our sickness." The help which Jesus rendered in all kinds of bodily sickness is taken in Matthew to be a fulfilment of what in Isaiah is prophesied of the Servant of Jehovah. The Hebrew verbs of the text, when used of sin, signify to assume as a heavy burden and bare away the guilt of sin as one's own; that is, to bear sin mediatorially in order to atone for it. But here, where, not sins, but our sicknesses and our pains are the object, the mediatorial sense remains the same. It is not meant that the Servant of Jehovah merely entered into fellowship of our sufferings, but that He took upon Himself the sufferings which we had to bear and deserved to bear; and therefore He not only bore them away, but also in His own Person endured them in order to discharge us from them.

Now, when one takes sufferings upon himself which another had to bear, and does this not merely in fellowship with him but in his stead, we call it substitution. *Here*, then, the best results of rigid exegesis show that the bearing and removal of human disease is an integral part of redeeming work, a provision of the Atonement, a part of the doctrine of Christ Crucified; that Jesus is the Savior of the body as well as of the spirit, and that

> He comes to make His blessings flow
> Far as the curse is found.

"Bodily healing by direct Divine agency becomes a boon for every believer in any period of Gospel history. It settles the question of a preacher's duty to preach it."

An Objection Answered

A Canadian writer objects that Matthew 8:17 cannot refer to the Atonement, because since Christ had not yet been crucified, this would be "making Christ live an atoning life." This, to me, is no argument at all, since Christ was "the Lamb of God slain from the foundation of the world." He not only healed disease before Calvary, but He also forgave sins, and yet both of these mercies were bestowed on the ground of the Atonement yet future.

A prominent New York clergyman raises practically the same objection. He argues that the fact that Christ, in Matthew, is fulfilling Isaiah's prophecy by healing the sick, proves that "Jesus bore our sickness not on the Cross, but when He was alive in the city of Capernaum." In answering this, I have only to ask, Did Jesus bear our *iniquities* in Capernaum or on the Cross? His forgiving of sins as well as His healing of the sick were both done with respect to His coming Atonement, because "without the shedding of blood there is no remission."

The prophecy states that "He hath borne *our* sicknesses." This includes all others, as well as those at Capernaum. In verses 4 and 5 of this Redemption Chapter, we see Him dying for

> *"OUR* sicknesses"
> *"OUR* pains"
> *"OUR* transgressions"
> *"OUR* iniquities"
> *"OUR* peace"
> *"OUR healing"* for "by His stripes we are healed."

We would have to misquote to exclude ourselves from any of these blessings.

The only "surely" in the Redemption Chapter prefaces His provision for our healing. There could be no stronger statement of our complete redemption from pain and sickness by His Atoning death. If Christ, as some think, is unwilling to heal as universally during His exaltation as He did during His humiliation, then He would have to break His promise in St. John 14:12,13, and He would not be "Jesus Christ, the same yesterday, today and forever."

The fact of healing in the Atonement *necessitates* the continuation of His healing ministry during His exaltation, because His redeeming work embraced all who live on earth while He is with the Father. Accordingly, He gives the above promise to do the same, and greater works, in answer to our prayers from God's right hand. As long as the Church remained under the control of the Spirit the same works continued, and history reveals, as Dr. A. J. Gordon puts it, "that whenever we find a revival of primitive faith and Apostolic simplicity, there we find the Evangelical miracles which surely characterize the Apostolic age."

The Apostle tells us, "He was made sin for us Who knew no sin" (of His own.) Likewise, "He hath made Him sick" (for us) Who knew no sickness (of His own.) Peter writes, "Who His own self bore our sins in His own body on the tree," and Isaiah declares, "Surely our sicknesses He hath borne, and our pains—He hath carried them." But, as Leeser translates, "only *our* sickness did He bear," having none of His own.

Again, in the 4th verse of Dr. Young's translation cited above, we read, "and Jehovah hath caused to meet on Him the punishment of us all." One writer inquires, on this point, "What are the punishments of sin?" and then says, in substance, all will admit that sin is punished by soul-condemnation, remorse, mental anxiety and frequently by sickness . . . and believe these are remitted because of vicarious Atonement. By what rule of Scripture or reason is the last-mentioned punishment severed from the rest? Mark the prophet's words, "Jehovah hath caused to meet on Him the *punishment* of us all." Since sickness is a part of that punishment, it is demonstrated by the immutable Word of God that sickness is included in the Atonement. He then asks, "Is it true that God will give deliverance from every penalty and consequence of sin *except one,* and that this one (sickness) must inevitably remain to the bitter end? Away with such a thought! Isaiah affirms that the *entire* punishment of us all was caused to meet on Him . . . He testified 'It is finished.' There was nothing incomplete about the work of our mighty Jesus." I might add to this that, were it otherwise, the prophet should have said, "Jehovah hath caused to meet on Him only a *part* of the punishment of us all."

The Cross a Perfect Remedy for the Whole Man

"Jesus went to the cross, spirit, soul and body, to redeem man, spirit, soul and body. Therefore, the Cross is the centre of the plan of salvation for man, spirit, soul and body."

Every form of sickness and disease known to man was included, and many of them even mentioned particularly, in the "curse of the law," (Deut. 28:15-62, and other scriptures.) Now, in Galatians 3:13, we have the positive statement that "Christ hath redeemed us from the curse of the law, being made a curse for us, for it is written, Cursed is every one that hangeth on the tree." What plainer declaration could we have than that Christ, Who was born under the law to redeem us, bore its curse, and therefore did redeem us from all sickness and disease. Here it is stated that it was on the cross that Jesus redeemed us from the law's curse. In other words, He redeemed us from the following diseases, specified in Deuteronomy, "consumption" (tuberculosis), "fever," "inflamation," "the botch of Egypt," "emerods," "scab," "itch," "madness" (insanity), "blindness," "plagues," "all the diseases of Egypt," "also every sickness and every plague which is not written in the book of this law." This would include cancer, influenza, mumps, measles and every other modern disease. If Christ redeemed us from the curse of the law, and sickness is included in the curse, surely He redeemed us from sickness.

Redemption Synonymous with Calvary

Redemption is synonymous with Calvary, therefore we are redeemed from the entire curse, body, soul and spirit, solely through His Atonement. Now, since disease is a part of the curse, how could God *justly* remove this part of the curse by healing the sick without first redeeming us from it? Again, since "Christ redeemed us from the curse of the law," how can God justify us and at the same time require us to remain under the law's curse, when, as the Apostle says, "ye are not under the law, but under grace"? (Romans 6:14) . In short, why should anyone remain under the law's curse who is not under the law? To do so, would be the same as putting a man in prison for life after he had been proven innocent and the court had justified him from the charge of murder.

Paul argues, in Romans the 3rd chapter, that "God set forth Christ to be a propitiation . . . that He might be just and the justifier of him which believeth in Jesus." In other words, were it not for the Atonement, God would be *unjust* in justifying the sinner; and likewise He would be unjust in healing the sick without first redeeming them from the sickness. The fact that God ever healed anyone is to me the best proof that healing was provided by the Atonement. If healing was not provided for all in redemption, how did all in the whole multitude obtain from Christ the healing that God did not provide? "He healed them *all.*"

An Important Question

If the body were not included in redemption, how can there be a resurrection? How can "corruption put on incorruption," or "mortal put on immortality?" If we have not been redeemed from sickness, would we not be subject to disease in Heaven, if it were possible to be resurrected irrespective of redemption? Some one has well remarked, "Man's future destiny being both spiritual and bodily, his redemption *must* be both spiritual and bodily."

Why should not the "last Adam" take away all that the "first Adam" brought upon us?

Now let us consider a few Gospel parallels.

"THE INNER MAN"

Adam, by his fall, brought sin into our souls.

Sin is therefore the work of the devil.

Jesus was "manifested to destroy the works of the devil" in the soul.

The redemptive name "JEHOVAH-TSIDKENU" reveals His redemptive provision for our souls.

On Calvary Jesus *"bare our sins."*

He was made "sin for us" (II Cor. 5:21) when "He bare our sins" (I Peter 2:24).

"Who His own self bare our sins in His body on the tree."

"Who forgiveth all thine iniquities."

"For ye are bought with a price: therefore glorify God in your . . . spirit."

The spirit is bought with a price.

Is remaining in sin the way to glorify God in your spirit?

Since He "bare *our* sins," how many *must* it be God's will to save, when they come to Him? "Whosoever believeth."

"THE OUTER MAN"

Adam, by his fall, brought disease into our bodies.

Disease is therefore the work of the devil. Jesus "went about doing good, and healing all that were oppressed *of the devil."*

Jesus was "manifested to destroy the works of the devil" in the body.

The redemptive name "JEHOVAH-RAPHA" reveals His redemptive provision for our bodies.

On Calvary Jesus *"bare our sicknesses."*

He was "made a curse for us" (Gal. 3:13) when He "bare our sicknesses" (Matt. 8:17).

"By whose stripes ye were healed."

"Who healeth all thy diseases."

"For ye are bought with a price: therefore glorify God in your body . . ." (I Cor. 6:20).

The body is bought with a price.

Is remaining sick the way to glorify God in your body?

Since He "bare *our* sicknesses," how many *must* it be God's will to heal, when they come to Him? "He healed them all."

"As God 'made Him to be sin for us who knew no sin.' "
—Rev. A. J. Gordon.

"So God made Him to be sick for us who knew no sickness."
—Rev. A. J. Gordon.

"Since our Substitute bore our sins, did He not do so that we might not bare them?"
—Rev. A. J. Gordon.

"Since our Substitute bore our sicknesses, did He not do so that we might not bare them?"
—Rev. A. J. Gordon.

"Christ bore our sins that we might be delivered from them. Not SYMPATHY—a suffering *with*, but SUBSTITUTION—a suffering *for*."
—Rev. A. J. Gordon.

Christ bore our sicknesses that we might be delivered from them. Not SYMPATHY—a suffering *with*, but SUBSTITUTION—a suffering *for*.

"If the fact that Jesus 'bore our sins in His own body on the tree' be a valid reason why we should all trust Him now for the forgiveness of our sins,

why is not the fact that He 'bore our sicknesses' an equally valid reason why we should all trust Him now to heal our bodies?" (Writer unknown).

Faith for salvation "cometh by hearing" the Gospel — He "bare our sins."

Faith for healing "cometh by hearing" — He "bare our sicknesses."

Therefore, Preach the Gospel (that He bore our sins) to every creature,"

and "the Gospel (that He bore our sicknesses) to every creature."

Christ's promise for the soul ("shall be saved") is in the great commission (Mark 16).

Christ's promise for the body ("shall recover") is in the great commission (Mark 16).

In connection with the ordinance of baptism, the Bible teaches that he that believeth and is baptized shall be saved (Mark 16).

In connection with the ordinance of anointing with oil, the Bible teaches that he that believeth and is anointed shall be healed (James 5:14).

We are commanded to baptize in Christ's name.

We are commanded to anoint "in the name of the Lord" (James 5:14).

In the Lord's Supper the wine is taken "in remembrance" of His death for our souls (I Cor. 11:25).

In the Lord's Supper the bread is eaten "in remembrance" of His death for our bodies (I Cor. 11:23-24).

The sinner is to repent before believing the Gospel "unto righteousness."

James 5:16 says, "Confess therefore, your sins . . . that ye may be healed."

Water baptism stands for total surrender and obedience.

Anointing with oil is the symbol and sign of consecration.

The sinner must accept God's promise as true before he can feel the joy of salvation.

The sick must accept God's promise as true before he can feel well.

"*As many* as received Him . . . were born . . . of God" (St. John 1:12-13).

"*As many* as touched Him were made whole" (Mark 6:56)

I will now cite one out of many hundreds of cases of sickness and affliction that have been healed while the sufferers listened to the preaching on the subject of healing in the Atonement. Their healing came through their own faith before having an opportunity of being anointed.

When but a child of eight years, Mrs. Clara Rupert of Lima, Ohio, had such a severe case of whooping-cough that she ruptured the muscles of one eye, leaving it entirely blind, and so dead that during all the years that followed she could rub her finger on the bare eyeball without pain. She said that on windy days, when particles would blow into the eye, it caused her no suffering.

Just Because the Bible Says So

While listening to a sermon on the Atonement, during our revival in Lima, Ohio, she said in her heart: "If that is true, and it is because the Bible says so, then I am just as sure of receiving sight in my blind eye tonight when I go to the altar as I was sure of salvation when I went to the Methodist altar several years ago and was saved. Accordingly, with this logical reasoning, she came to the altar, and while we were praying with others she asked God to heal her. Before we had a chance to anoint her, she was on her feet weeping, and walked back and threw her arms around her father's neck, the audience wondering why she left the altar without being anointed. Her father said: "What is the matter, daughter?" and she replied, "My eye!" He said: "Why, is it paining you?" She said: "No, I can see perfectly!"

A few months later, while we were holding a revival in St. Paul, Minn., we met this woman and her husband, who were there attending the Bible school, preparing for work for the Master. Her husband wanted to preach the Gospel of Christ, Who had so graciously healed his wife.

Almost daily in our revivals testimonies are given by those who have been healed while sitting in their seats listening to the Gospel.

What Eminent Men Have to Say

These views on healing in the Atonement are not new and peculiar only to myself. Many of the most godly and able teachers of the Church have seen and taught them. In addition to those teachers already quoted, I will add a few words from Dr. Torrey and others.

Dr. R. A. Torrey, in his book on "Divine Healing" declares: "The atoning death of Jesus Christ secured for us not only physical healing, but the resurrection and perfecting and glorifying of our bodies . . . The Gospel of Christ has salvation for the body as well as for the soul . . . Just as one gets the first-fruits of his spiritual salvation in the life that now is, so we get the first-fruits of our physical salvation in the life that now is . . . Individual believers, whether Elders or not, have the privilege and the duty to 'pray one for another' in case of sickness with the expectation that God will hear and heal."

Dr. R. E. Stanton, a former moderator of the General Assembly of the Presbyterian Church, gives the following in his Gospel Parallelisms: "It is my aim to show that the Atonement of Christ lays the foundation equally for deliverance from sin and for deliverance from disease. That complete provision has been made for both; that in the exercise of faith under the conditions prescribed, we have the same reason to believe that the body may be delivered from sickness that we have that the soul shall be delivered from sin; in short, that both branches of the deliverance stand on the same ground, and that it is necessary to include both in any true conception of what the gospel offers to mankind. The atoning sacrifice of Christ covers the physical as well as the spiritual needs of the race . . . Healing of the body is not, therefore, a 'side-issue,' as some represent it. It is no more this than the healing of the soul is a 'side-issue.' They are both but parts of the same Gospel, based equally upon the same great Atonement."

The Episcopal Church on Divine Healing

In the report of the Commission on spiritual healing appointed by the Episcopal Church, sponsored by Bishop Reese, who for many years has practiced the healing ministry, and who was Chairman of the Commission, is the following statement: "The healing of the body is an essential element of the Gospel, and must be preached and practiced . . . God wills our health, that the Church, the 'Body of Christ,' has the same commission and the same power as

'The Head,' that we churchmen, with this true conception of God as Creative Love, must now give a sinning and suffering world this full Gospel of salvation from sin and its inevitable consequences."

These conclusions were arrived at by this scholarly Commission after three years of study and research.

Bishop Charles H. Brent of the Episcopal Church, who as Head of all Chaplains in France, led the religious life of our armies overseas, affirms: "He who waives away the healing power of Christ as belonging only to the New Testament times is not preaching the whole Gospel. God was, and Is, the Saviour of the body as well as the soul."

James Moore Hickson pleads: "A living Church is one in which the Living Christ lives and walks, doing through its members what He did in the days of His flesh. It must, therefore, be a *healing* Church as well as a soul-saving Church . . . Spiritual healing is sacramental. It is the extension through the members of His mystical body of His own incarnate life."

The late able writers, Dr. A. B. Simpson, Andrew Murray, A. T. Pierson, Dr. A. J. Gordon, and many present writers whom we might quote, have been teachers of healing in the Atonement. An unknown writer has said: "On the cross of Calvary Jesus has nailed the proclamation, *'Deliver from going down to the pit (grave) for I have found an Atonement'* " (Job 33:24).

Isaiah begins the Redemption Chapter with the question "Who hath believed our report, and to whom is the arm of the Lord revealed?" And the report follows that He bore our sins and sicknesses. The answer to the question is, only those who have heard the report could believe it, because "faith cometh by hearing." Since Jesus died to save and to heal it is surely worth reporting.

The purpose of this sermon is to prove that healing is provided by the Atonement and is therefore a part of the Gospel which Christ commanded to be preached

> To "all the world,"
> To "all nations,"
> To "every creature,"
> With "all Power,"
> Throughout "all the days,
> Even unto the end of the (present) age."

3

Is Healing For All?

Is it still the will of God, as in the past, to heal all who have need of healing, and to fulfil the number of their days?

The greatest barrier to the faith of many seeking bodily healing in our day is the uncertainty in their minds as to it being the will of God to heal *all*. Nearly every one knows that God does heal *some*, but there is much in modern theology that keeps the people from knowing what the Bible clearly teaches—that healing is provided for all. It is impossible to boldly claim by fatih a blessing which we are not sure God offers, because the power of God can be claimed only where the will of God is known.

It would be next to impossible to get a sinner to "believe unto righteousness" before you had fully convinced him that it was God's will to save *him*. Faith begins where the will of God is known. If it is God's will to heal only *some* of those who need healing, then none have any basis for faith unless they have a special revelation that they are among the favored ones. Faith must rest on the will of God alone, not on our desires or wishes. Appropriating faith is not believing that God *can* but that God *will*. Because of not knowing it to be a redemptive privilege for *all*, most of those in our day, when seeking healing, add to their petition the phrase, "If it be Thy will."

40

A Corrected Theology

Among all those who sought healing from Christ during
His earthly ministry, we read of only one who had this kind
of theology. This was the leper, who said, "Lord, *if Thou
wilt,* Thou canst make me clean." The first thing Christ
did was to correct his theology by saying, "*I will,* be thou
clean." Christ's "I will" cancelled his "*if,*" adding to his
faith that Christ *could* heal him, the faith that He *would.*

The theology of this leper, before Christ enlightened
him, is almost universal today, because this part of the gospel is so seldom and so fragmentarily preached.

We see, from almost every conceivable angle throughout
the Scriptures, that there is no doctrine more clearly taught
than that it *is* God's will to heal *all* who have need of
healing, and that they may fulfil the number of their days,
according to His promise. Of course, we mean all who are
properly taught and who meet the conditions prescribed in
the Word. Now I hear someone say, "If healing is for all
then we shall never die." Why not? Divine healing goes no
further than the promise of God. He does not promise that
we shall never die, but He says, "I will take sickness away
from the midst of thee . . . the number of thy days I will
fulfil" (Ex. 23:25, 26).

"The days of our years are threescore years and ten"
(Psa. 90:10).
"Take me not away in the midst of my days"
(Psa. 102:24).
"Why shouldst thou die before thy time?" (Eccl. 7:17)

Then some one may ask, Well, how is a man going to die?
"Thou takest away their breath, they die, and return to
their dust" (Psa. 104:29).

The Rev. P. Gavin Duffy writes on this point, "He has
allotted to man a certain span of life, and His will is that

life shall be lived out. I want you to recall that all those
He called back from the dead were *young people* who had not
lived out their fulness of years; and in that very fact we may
well see His protest against premature death . . . Of course,
we must not expect that the old shall be physically young,
but if the alloted span has not been spent we have a right
to claim God's gift of health; and, even though it be past,
if it be His Will that we should continue here for a time
longer, it is equally His Will that we should do so in good
health."

> Death comes, and then we blame our God,
>   And weakly say, "Thy will be done";
> But never underneath the sod
>   Has God imprisoned any one.
> God does not send disease, or crime,
>   Or carelessness, or fighting clans;
> And when we die before our time,
>   The fault is man's.
>
> He is a God of life, not death;
>   He is one God that gives us birth;
> He has not shortened by a breath
>   The life of any on the earth;
> And He would have us dwell within
>   The world our full allotted years.
> So blame not God—for our own sin
>   Makes our own tears.
>
>   *Douglas Malloch*

Read the Will and Know

If we would know what is in a will, let us read the will.
If we want to know God's will on any subject, let us read His
will. Suppose a lady should say, "My husband, who was very
rich, has passed away; now, I wish I knew whether he left me
anything in the will." I would say to her, "Why don't you
read the will and see?" The word "testament," legally speak-

ing, means a person's will. The Bible contains God's last will and testament, in which He bequeaths to us all the blessings of redemption; and since it is His *"last* will and testament," anything later is a forgery. A man never writes a new will after he is dead. If healing is in God's will for us, then to say that the age of miracles is past is virtually saying what is the opposite of the truth, that a will is no good after the death of the testator. Jesus is not only the testator, who died; He was resurrected, and is also the mediator of the will. He is our lawyer, so to speak, and He will not beat us out of the Will, as some earthly lawyers do. He is our Representative at the right hand of God.

For the answer to the question under consideration, let us look away from modern tradition and go to the Word of God, which is a revelation of His will.

In the 15th chapter of Exodus, just after the passage of the Red sea, which typified our redemption, and "was written for our admonition," God gave His first promise to heal. This promise was for *all.* God named the conditions, the conditions were met, and we read: "He brought them forth also with silver and gold, and there was not one feeble person among all their tribes." It is here that God gave the covenant of healing, revealed by and sealed with His first covenant and Redemptive name, *Jehovah-Rapha,* translated, "I am the Lord that healeth thee." This is God's word, "settled in heaven," a never-changing fact concerning God.

Who Is Authorized to Change God's Will?

To say that this privilege of health is not for God's people today, is to change God's "I *Am*" to "I *Was*" Jehovah-Rapha. Who has the authority to change God's Redemptive names? Instead of abandoning His office as Healer, He is "Jesus Christ, the same yesterday, today, and forever," under this first covenant name, as well as under the other six. The blessings revealed by His Redemptive names, as we have seen in the preceding sermon, were provided by the Atonement, when He "tasted death *for every man*," and therefore cannot be confined to Israel. This 15th chapter of Exodus shows us that at least in that age of the world, 3500 years ago, God did not leave the people in doubt concerning His willingness to heal *all*.

A Nation Without One Feeble Person

This universal state of health in the nation of Israel continued as long as God's conditions were met. Then, twenty years later (Numbers 16:46-50) when, because of sin the plague destroyed 14,700, they again met conditions, the plague was stayed, and He was still Jehovah-Rapha, the Healer, not to some, but to *all*. It would not be true that the plague was stayed if it remained on even one of them. This state of health again remained uninterrupted until nineteen years later, when the people, not satisfied with God's way for them, chosen in love and mercy, spake against God and against Moses, and they were cursed with the fiery serpents. When they again met God's conditions, by confessing their sins, His word through Moses to them was, "It shall come to pass that *every one* that is bitten, when he looketh upon it (the type of Calvary) shall live." So, again, at this time, the Scriptures show us that it was still God's will to heal, not some, but *all*. *Every one* that was bitten lived by beholding the brazen serpent, which was a typical foreshadowing of the coming sacrifice upon Calvary in our behalf.

The Psalmist David, in his time, understood healing to be a universal privilege. In the 86th Psalm he says, "For thou, Lord, art good . . . plenteous in mercy unto *all* them that call upon Thee." We shall see, in the following sermon, that healing was one of the most prominent mercies throughout the Scriptures, and that the sick, in the New Testament, asked for "mercy" when seeking healing from Christ; for God's mercy covers man's physical, as well as spiritual nature. Therefore, Jesus, according to the Old Testament promise, showed that He was "plenteous in mercy," by healing, not *some,* but *all* who came to Him. Again, in the 103rd Psalm, we see that David believed that the mercy of healing was as universal a privilege as the mercy of forgiveness. He calls upon his soul to bless God, "Who forgiveth *all* thine iniquities, Who healeth *all* thy diseases." "Who healeth *all*" is as permanent as "Who forgiveth *all,*" for the identical language is used with reference to both mercies.

In the 91st Psalm, God says concerning the man "that dwelleth in the secret place of the Most High . . . *with long life will I satisfy him.*" Is the privilege of dwelling in the secret place only for a few or for all? If it is for all, then God's promise to *all* is, "With long life will I satisfy him." God would have to break this promise to be unwilling to heal His obedient children in middle life. If dwelling in the secret place was possible in a darker age of the world, surely it is in this better age of grace, during which "He is able to make all grace abound" towards each of His children. The holy prophets of the Old Testament "prophesied of the grace that should come to *us.*"

Calvary Meets All Man's Needs

We have seen, in the great Redemption Chapter, the 53rd of Isaiah, that it is *our* sicknesses, as well as *our* sins that Jesus bore, making one privilege as universal as the other. What Jesus did for individuals who came to Him for blessings was for *them,* but what He did on Calvvary was for *all.*

It is clear that in all of these instances cited from the Old Testament it was God's will to heal *all* who met the conditions. Wherever forgiveness was offered, healing was also offered. Let those who teach the people that God's will in the matter of healing is not the same today answer the question, "Why would God withdraw this Old Testament mercy from this better dispensation?" Is it not to be expected that He, Who "hath reserved better things for us" and Who is "the same yesterday, today, and forever" should continue these same mercies throughout this better dispensation? Let us now look in the New Testament and see.

Christ the Expression of God's Will

There is no better way of ascertaining the proper answer to the question before us than by reading the Gospels, which record the teachings and the works of Christ. He was the expression of the Father's will. His life was both a revelation and a manifestation of the unchanging love and will of God. He literally acted out the will of God for Adam's race. He said, "I came down from heaven, not to do my will, but the will of Him that sent Me," and that "the Father that dwelleth in Me, He doeth the works." He also said, "He that hath seen Me hath seen the Father," therefore, when He healed the multitudes who thronged Him, day after day, we see the Father revealing His will. When "He laid His hands on *every one* of them, and healed them" He was doing and revealing the will of God for *our* bodies. Perhaps no one would be more conservative than the scholars of the Episcopalian church, and yet, the commission appointed to study the subject of spiritual healing and report back to the church, after three years of study and research in both the Bible and history, say in their report, "The healing of the sick by Jesus was done as a revelation of God's will for man." Because they discovered that His will is fully revealed, they further say,

"No longer can the Church pray for the sick with the *faith-destroying*, qualifying phrase 'If it be Thy will.' "

The message everywhere taught in the Gospels is one of complete healing for soul and body for all who come to Him. Many today say, "I believe in healing, but I do not believe it is for every one." If it is not, how could we pray the prayer of faith for *any*, or even for one whom it is God's will to heal, until we have a revelation by the Spirit that we are praying for the right one? If it is not God's will to heal *all*, then no man can ascertain the will of God for himself from the Bible. Are we to understand from these teachers that we must close our Bibles and get our revelation direct from the Spirit, before we can pray for the sick, because the will of God cannot be ascertained from the Scriptures?

This would be virtually teaching that the whole of the Divine activity on the line of healing would have to be governed by the direct revelation of the Spirit, instead of by the Scriptures. How are the sick to be healed if there is no Gospel (good news) of healing to proclaim to them as a basis for their faith? Or, since faith is expecting God to keep His promise, how can there be faith for healing if there is no promise in the Bible that the sick can apply to himself? The Scriptures tell us how God heals the sick. "He sendeth His *Word* and healeth them and delivereth them from their graves" (Psa. 107:20). " . . . the *word* of God which effectually worketh" in them that believe, and is "health to all their flesh." (See I Thess. 2:12; Prov. 4:22).

Faith Rests on More Than Mere Ability

If a millionaire were to appear before an audience of a thousand people, with the announcement that he was able to give each one a thousand dollars, this would be no basis for any to have faith for a thousand dollars, because faith cannot rest on ability. If he should go further, and say, "I will give fifty of you a thousand dollars each," even then there is no basis for any one in the audience to have faith for the thousand dollars. Were you to ask one of them if he or she were "fully assured" of receiving a thousand dollars from the millionaire, the answer would be, "I need the money, and hope I am among the lucky ones, but I cannot be sure." But, should the millionaire say, "*It is my will* to give all a thousand dollars each," then every one in the audience would have a ground for faith, and would undoubtedly say to the rich man, "Thank you! I'll take my money."

Now, supposing God were a respecter of persons, and that it was His will to heal only *some* of those who need healing, let us take a glance through the Gospels, and see how the friends of the sick decided which of the sick to bring to Him for healing. "Now, when the sun was setting, *all* they that had *any* sick with divers diseases, brought them unto Him; and He laid His hands on *every one* of them and healed them" (Luke 4:40). Here the unlucky ones, if there were any, were brought, and all healed the same as the others. Surely, it was God *doing* and *revealing* His own will. If you had been there and were sick, you would have been brought, and would have been healed with the rest, because they brought them *all*. Matthew, in his record of this same instance, tells why Jesus made no exceptions. "He healed them all, that it might be fulfilled which was spoken by Esaias, the prophet, saying, "Himself took *our* infirmities and bare *our* sicknesses." The word "our" means everybody, in the sacrifice of Calvary, and it therefore requires the healing of *all*, to fulfil the prophecy. Not only on this occasion, but on every occasion since, down until today, He heals the sick "that it might be fulfilled which was spoken by Esaias, the Prophet, saying, Himself took *our* infirmities and bare *our* sicknesses."

Let the sick go through the Gospels and note the *all's* and the *every's* and they will see that the redemptive blessing of healing was for *all*, and that no one ever appealed in vain to Jesus for healing. There never was a multitude large enough to have in it even one that Jesus wanted to remain sick, and would not heal.

Jesus Healed Everything and All

"And Jesus went about all Galilee, teaching . . . and preaching the Gospel . . . and healing *all manner* of sicknesses, and *all manner* of disease among the people. And His fame went throughout all Syria; and they brought unto Him *all* sick people that were taken with divers diseases and torments, and those which were possessed with devils, and those which were lunatic, and those that had the palsy; *and He healed them all* — (Moffat's translation) . . . And there followed Him great multitudes of people from Galilee, and from Decapolis, and from Jerusalem, and from Judea, and from beyond Jordan" (Matt. 4:23-25) .

"And Jesus went about all the cities and villages teaching . . . and preaching the Gospel . . . and healing *every* sickness and *every disease* among the people. But when He saw the multitudes He was moved with compassion on them . . . And when He had called unto Him His twelve disciples He gave them power against unclean spirits to cast them out and to heal *all manner* of sickness and *all manner* of disease" (Matt. 9:35 to Matt. 10:1) .

Note, here, that it was the multitudes coming for healing that necessitated the thrusting forth of new laborers into His harvest to preach and to heal. It was not long until seventy more were needed, and were sent forth to heal as well as to preach.

"But when Jesus knew it, He withdrew Himself from thence, and *great multitudes* followed Him, *and He healed them all*" (Matt. 12:15) .

"And Jesus went forth and saw a *great multitude*, and was moved with compassion toward them, and healed their sick" (Matt. 14:14).

"And when they were gone over they came into the land of Gennesaret, and when the men of that place had knowledge of Him they sent out into all that country round about, and brought unto Him *all that were diseased;* and besought Him that they might only touch the hem of His garment, and as many as touched were made perfectly whole" (Matt. 14:34-36).

"And a *great multitude* of the people out of all Judea and Jerusalem, and from the coast of Tyre and Sidon, which came to hear Him, and to be healed of their diseases and they that were vexed with unclean spirits, and they were healed, and the *whole multitude* sought to touch Him for there went virtue out of Him, and healed them *all*" (Luke 6:17-19).

We see throughout the Gospels that, in bringing the sick to Christ for healing, it was repeatedly stated that they brought them *all*, which included all the unlucky ones if there were any. If, according to modern tradition, it is God's will for the sick to patiently remain so for His glory, is it not strange that there should not be even one of this class in all these multitudes brought to Christ for healing? By healing the epileptic (Mark 9:14-29) Jesus proved it to be the Father's will to heal even this one whom the disciples, divinely commissioned to cast out demons failed to deliver. We see by this verse that it would have been wrong to call in question and to teach God's unwillingness to heal because of this failure on the part of the disciples. Jesus, by healing him, shows them that the failure proved nothing but unbelief. Peter, after three years of constant association with the Lord, describes His earthly ministry in this one brief statement: "God anointed Jesus of Nazareth with the Holy Ghost and with Power, Who went about doing good, and healing *all* that were oppressed of the devil, for God was with Him" (Acts 10:38) .

So, in all the above, and many other Scriptures which show He healed them *all,* we have the will of God revealed for our bodies, and the answer to the question, "Is healing for all?"

Compassionate Love Jesus' Ruling Motive

Many, in our day, have been taught that Christ performed miracles of healing just to show His power and to prove His deity. This may be true, but it is far from being *all* the truth. He would not have had to heal *all* to show His power; a few outstanding cases would prove this. But the Scriptures show that he healed because of His compassion and to fulfil prophecy. Others teach that He healed the sick to make Himself known, but in Matt. 12:15, 16, we read, "Great multitudes followed Him, and He healed them *all,* and charged them that they should *not make Him known."*

Some, who have to admit that Jesus healed all who came to Him, hold that Isaiah's prophecy concerning His bearing our sicknesses refers only to His earthly ministry; that this universal manifestation of His compassion was special, and not a revelation of the unchanging will of God. But the Bible clearly teaches that He only *"began to do and teach"* what was not only to be continued, but augmented, after His ascension.

After Christ, for three years, had healed all that came to Him, He said, "It is expedient (profitable) for you that I go away."

How could this be true if His going away would modify His ministry to the afflicted?

Anticipating the unbelief with which this wonderful promise would be regarded, He prefaced His promise to continue the same and greater works in answer to our prayers after His exaltation, with the words "Verily, verily." "Verily, verily, I say unto you, he that believeth on Me, the works that I do shall he do also; and greater works than these shall he do, because I go unto My Father, and (how are we to do them?) whatsoever ye ask the Father in My name that will *I* do, that the Father may be glorified in the Son" (John 14:12, 13).

In other words, we are to do them by asking *Him* to do them.

He did not say "less works," but *"the* works" and *"greater* works."

To me, this promise from the lips of Christ is a complete answer to all opposers and to all their books and articles against Divine healing.

"It is written" was Christ's policy when resisting the devil.

Wm. Jennings Bryan well asks, "Since Christ said 'It is written,' and the devil said 'It is written,' why can't the preacher say 'It is written?' "

The Wisdom of the Early Church

The early Church took Christ at His word and prayed unitedly for signs and wonders of healing, until "the place was shaken where they were assembled together," and then "they brought forth the sick into the streets and laid them on beds and couches . . . There came also a multitude out of the cities round about Jerusalem, bringing sick folks, and they which were vexed with unclean spirits, and they were *healed every one."* "All that Jesus *began* to do and to teach" He was here continuing from the right hand of God through "His Body, the Church," according to His promise. Some say, "Oh, that was only in the beginning of the Acts, for the purpose of confirming their word regarding Christ's resurrection."

Let us, then, turn to the *last* chapter of Acts, and read how, thirty years later, after Paul, on the island of Melita, had healed the father of Publius, "All the other sick people in the island came, and were cured." (Weymouth.)

So we see, again, at this time, in the very last chapter of the Acts of the Holy Ghost, which is the only unfinished book of the New Testament, it is still the will of God to heal; not some, but *all*.

The Acts of the Holy Ghost

The Holy Spirit, Whom Christ sent as His Successor and Executive, took possession of the Church, which is the Body of Christ, and showed the same healing power *after* Pentecost that Christ had displayed *before,* and vast multitudes were healed. As in the Gospels, so in the Acts, we never read of any one asking for healing and being denied. Men have named this book the "Acts of the Apostles." A better and a truer name for this book would be "The Acts of the Holy Ghost," because it records the acts of the Holy Ghost through others as well as the Apostles. Phillip and Stephen, who were not Apostles, were as gloriously used as Peter and John. The Holy Spirit came to execute for us all the blessings purchased by Christ's redemption, and pledged by the seven redemptive names. He has never lost any of His interest in the work He came to do. If you wish to know how He wants to act *today,* read how He did act. The book of Acts shows us how He wants to act throughout "all the days, even unto the end of the age."

It was the Holy Spirit Who worked all the miracles of healing at the hands of Christ. Jesus never undertook a miracle until, in answer to His prayer, the Holy Spirit, the Miracle-Worker, came upon Him, and then, in full reliance upon the Spirit, He cast out devils and healed the sick. The miracles of Christ were all done by the Spirit in advance of His own dispensation, or before He had yet entered officially into office. Why would the Holy Spirit, Who healed *all* the sick before His dispensation began, do less after He entered office? Did the Miracle-Worker enter office to do away with miracles during His own dispensation?

Is the teaching and the practice of the Church in the matter of healing in this Laodicean (lukewarm) period of her history a truer expression of the will of God than the teaching and practice of the early Church while under the full sway of the Spirit? Decidedly not! I hesitate not to say that modern theology has robbed the Holy Spirit of a part of His ministry.

Now, in summing up what we have thus far written, we have a revelation from many angles of

Christ's Merciful Attitude Toward Our Sicknesses and Infirmities Since His Exaltation at the Right Hand of God

We deal now, not with the past, but only with Christ's *present* attitude towards sickness and disease.

1. Christ's present attitude is fully revealed by His redemptive name Jehovah-Rapha. His redemptive names cannot change. All will admit that His *other* six redemptive names are a revelation of His *present* attitude in the matter of bestowing the blessing that each name was given to reveal. By what logic, then, can we suppose that He has abandoned His office as Healer, revealed by the name Jehovah-Rapha?

2. His present attitude is again fully revealed by His own definite promise to continue and augment His healing ministry in answer to the prayer of believers while He is at the right hand of God. "Verily, verily, I say unto you, he that believeth on Me, *the works* that I do shall he do also; and *greater works* than these shall ye do, because I go unto My Father. And

whatsoever ye shall ask in My name that will I do that the Father may be glorified in the Son" (St. John 14:12, 13).

3. His present attitude is revealed by His own fulfilment of the above promise, recorded in the Book of Acts. Even in the very last chapter, 30 years after His ascension, we read, *"All the other sick people in the island came and were cured"* (Acts 28:9, Weymouth).

4. His present attitude is revealed by the fact that healing is a part of the Gospel that Christ commanded to be preached

To "all the world"

To "all nations"

To "every creature"

Throughout "all the days"

Even unto the end of the (present) age."

This commission is followed by the promise "they shall lay hands on the sick and they shall recover."

5. His present attitude is revealed by the fact that His substitutionary work on Calvary was in behalf of all those who live on earth during His exaltation at the right hand of the Father. We have seen in the preceding sermon that, as in Leviticus it is recorded that all disease was healed on the ground of Atonement, so Matthew tells us that the Atonement was Christ's reason for making no exceptions in healing the sick who came to Him.

6. His present attitude is revealed by the plain command to "any sick" in the Church, while He is with the Father, to ask for anointing and prayer with the promise "the Lord shall raise him up" (James 5:14). Does He mean we shall pray with faith or without it? How can we pray "the prayer of faith" unless it is His will to heal; or, does He command us to pray for a thing He will not do? Right here, even laymen are commanded to confess their faults one to another and

pray one for the other, for healing, with the purpose that
Elijah prayed for rain (James 5:16-18).

Would God command us to thus importune for what it is
not His will to do? Certainly not!

7. His present attitude is revealed by the fact that it is since
His exaltation that He "set" (established) in the Church
teachers, miracles, gifts of healing, etc., for the continuance of
the "same works" and "greater works" which He promised He
would continue from God's right hand. History records the
manifestation of these miraculous gifts since the days of the
apostles down to the present time.

The Unchangeable Compassion of Jesus

8. His present attitude toward our sickness is wonderfully
revealed by the fact that since His exaltation, His compassion
has neither been withdrawn nor modified.

In a later sermon, on the subject of the Lord's compassion,
we shall see that during the earthly ministry of our Lord He
was everywhere *"moved with compassion* and healed *all* that
had need of healing." The same Greek word that is translated
"mercy" is also repeatedly translated "compassion," for they
are the same. When two blind men asked for mercy, Jesus
was moved with compassion and healed them.

Since bodily healing, in the New Testament, is everywhere
a mercy (it being mercy, or compassion, that moved Him to
heal all that came to Him), is not the promise still true that
He is "plenteous in mercy unto *all* that call" upon Him? Does
not this glorious Gospel dispensation proffer as much mercy
and compassion to its sufferers as did the darker dispensation?
The Rev. Kenneth Mackenzie, a noted teacher and writer of
the Episcopal church, asks on this point, "Could the loving
heart of the Son of God, Who had compassion upon the sick,

and healed all who had need of healing, cease to regard the sufferings of His own when He had become exalted at the right hand of the Father?"

An Absurd Feature of Modern Theology

Is it not strange that any one in this better age of grace should take a position which would be synonymous with saying that the manifestation of Christ's compassion to the afflicted has been withdrawn, or even modified, since His glorification? If God is not as willing to show the mercy of healing to His *worshippers* as He is to show the mercy of forgiveness to His *enemies,* then He is more willing to show mercy to the devil's children than His own. The Scriptures deny this by saying, "The mercy (compassion) of the Lord is from everlasting to everlasting (not upon the sinner alone, but) upon *them that fear Him,*" for He loves His own sick and suffering child even more than He loves the sinner. Thank God "His mercy (compassion) is unto all generations."

9. His present attitude is revealed by the fact that, in the Old Testament year of Jubilee, which Jesus, in the 4th chapter of Luke, applies to the Gospel era, it was *"every man"* who was told to return to his possession. As in the year of Jubilee its blessings were for *"every man,"* so in the Gospel era, its blessings are for *"every creature."* This is more fully developed in the preceding sermon.

10. His present attitude is also revealed by the fact that "He hath redeemed *us* (all of us) from the curse of the law" (Gal. 3:13). We have seen in the preceding sermon that this curse included all the diseases known to history. How can God justify us and at the same time require us to remain under the curse from which He redeemed us?

The Earnest of Complete Redemption

11. His present attitude is revealed by the fact that the Holy Spirit and His work in us is "The earnest of our inheritance until the redemption of the purchased possession" (Eph. 1:14). We have already pointed out that because our eternal destiny is both spiritual and bodily, our redemption also *must* be. Therefore we cannot receive our *full* inheritance until the coming Day of Redemption, but, thank God, by being filled with the Spirit, *we* now have the *"earnest"* of it. Paul tells us, "We *have* the firstfruits of the Spirit," and these are manifested both spiritually and physically. The "firstfruits of the Spirit" include the earnest of immortality, which is a foretaste of the resurrection. Since our bodies are members of Christ, His glorified bodily life is as truly linked with our bodies, as His spiritual life is linked with our spirits. The same life that is in the vine is in its branches; and in Christ, "the True Vine," there is both spiritual and bodily life. It is only by bringing into our bodies some of the same life that He is to bring at the resurrection that the Spirit *can* be the earnest of our inheritance to the body. Since our inheritance includes a glorified body, what must the Earnest be? Thank God, "the life also of Jesus" may "be made manifest in our mortal flesh"—*immortal* life touching our *mortal* bodies with a foretaste of redemption, to enable us to finish our course, in order that we may "receive a full reward."

12. Does not nature itself reveal the present attitude of Christ toward the healing of our bodies? Nature everywhere is healing, or at least doing her best to heal. As soon as disease germs enter our bodies, nature begins to expel them. Break a bone, or cut a finger, and nature will do her utmost to heal, and usually succeeds. Now, has God commanded nature to rebel against His own will? If sickness is the will of God for His children, would it not seem that He has?

God's Use of Bodily Affliction

If sickness, as some think, is the will of God for His faithful children, then it is a sin for them even to desire to be well, to say nothing of spending thousands of dollars to defeat His purpose. I truly thank God for all the help that has ever come to sufferers through the physician, through the surgeon, the hospital and the trained nurse; but, if sickness is the will of God, then, to quote one writer, "Every physician is a law-breaker; every trained nurse is defying the Almighty; every hospital is a house of rebellion, instead of a house of mercy," and, instead of *supporting* hospitals, we ought to do our utmost to *close* every one."

If the modern theology of those who teach that God wants some of His worshipers to remain sick for His glory is true, then Jesus, during His earthly ministry, never hesitated to rob the Father of all the glory He could by healing *all* who came to Him. The Holy Spirit, likewise, robbed Him of all the glory He could by healing all the sick in the streets of Jerusalem. And Paul, too, robbed God of all the glory he could by healing *all* the sick on the island of Melita.

Many today hold that God afflicts even the obedient, because He loves them, making sickness a love-token from our Heavenly Father. If this is true, why do they try to get rid of His love-token? Why does not the one suffering with a cancer pray for the second blessing for themselves and also ask Him to thus bless wife, children, father, mother, neighbors, etc?

Does not God sometimes chasten His people through sickness? Decidedly yes! When we disobey God, sickness may be permitted, through the Father's loving discipline; but God has told us just how it may be avoided and averted. "If we would judge ourselves we should not be judged, but when we are judged we are chastened of the Lord, that we should not be condemned with the world" (I Cor. 11:31, 32). These chastenings come to save us from final judgment; but when we see the cause of the chastening, and turn from it, God promises it shall be withdrawn. As soon as "we judge ourselves," or learn our lesson, the absolute promise is "we shall not be judged." By self-judgment we may avoid chastening. Divine healing is not unconditionally promised to all christians, regardless of their conduct. It is for those who believe and obey. "All the paths of the Lord are *mercy* and truth unto *such* as keep His Covenant and His testimonies" (Psa. 25:10).

13. His attitude now is shown by the fact that "He was manifested to destroy the works of the devil" (I John 3:8). Think of His leaving heaven and making the awful transition of becoming a man, and of all the suffering and sacrifice that followed. What was the purpose that moved Him in all this? The Scriptures give the answer—"For *this* purpose . . . that He might destroy the works of the devil." This purpose includes the healing of *"all* that were oppressed of the devil" (Acts 10:38). Since He was glorified has He relinquished this purpose, which He retained even during the bloody sweat of Gethsemane and the awful tortures of Calvary? Does He want the works of the devil that He formerly wanted to destroy to remain in our bodies? Can it be that He now wants a cancer, a "plague," a "curse," "the works of the devil," in "the members of Christ," and "the temples of the Holy Ghost?" Is it not His will to heal any part of "the Body of Christ?" If not, why has He commanded "any sick" in it to be anointed *in His name* for healing?

Since "the Body is for the Lord," a "living sacrifice unto God," would He not rather have a well body than one that is a wreck? If not, how can He make us "perfect in every good work to do His will?" Is God's expressed will that we "may abound unto every good work," that we may be "prepared unto every good work," "throughly furnished unto all good works," "zealous of good works," and "careful to maintain good works" only for well men and women? If for all, He would have to heal the sick to make this possible, because no man can "abound unto every good work" while confined to a sick room.

Salvation All-Inclusive

14. His present attitude is revealed in the very meaning of the word "salvation." The word *soteria*, which is the Greek word for salvation, implies deliverance, preservation, healing, health, soundness, and, in the New Testament is applied sometimes to the soul, and at other times to the body only. The Greek word *"sozo"* translated "saved," also means "healed," "made sound," "made whole." In Romans 10:9 it is translated "saved," and in Acts 14:9 the same word is translated "healed" in referring to the healing of the man lame from birth. Both Greek words for "salvation" and "saved" mean both spiritual and physical salvation; or, in other words, spiritual and physical healing. Paul, in Eph. 5:23, states, "He is the Savior of the body."

Is this for some, or for all?

Dr. Scofield, in his foot-note on the word "salvation" says, "Salvation is the great inclusive word of the Gospel, gathering into itself all the redemptive acts and processes." The word therefore, includes our possession and enjoyment of all the blessings revealed by His seven redemptive names; in fact, these names were given to show what our *salvation* includes. It is therefore the Gospel of healing for the body, as well as for the soul, which "is the power of God unto salvation to *every one* that believeth; to the Jew first, and *also to the Greek.*" "The same Lord over *all* is rich unto *all* that call upon Him."

4

The Lord's Compassion

"The Lord is gracious, and full of compassion;
slow to anger, and of great mercy. The Lord is good
to all: and His tender mercies are over all His works"
                                    (PSA. 145:8,9).

In the study of the Lord's compassion, we have, to my mind,
a complete revelation of the Lord's willingness to heal. During His earthly ministry He was everywhere *moved with compassion,* and healed all "them that had need of healing"; and
it is "this same Jesus" who, after saying, "It is expedient for
you that I go away," is now seated at the right hand of God,
"that He might be a merciful (compassionate) and faithful
High Priest" for us.

In the Scriptures, "compassion" and "mercy" mean the
same. The Hebrew noun, *rachamin,* is translated both
"mercy" and "compassion." The Greek verb, *eleeo,* is translated "have mercy" and "have compassion"; and, likewise,
the Greek adjective *eleemon* is defined "merciful—compassionate."

To have compassion is *to love tenderly, to pity, to show
mercy, to be full of eager yearning.*

God Nothing So Much As Love

The text above begins with "the Lord is gracious and full
of compassion." These sentiments concerning the nature of
God are expressed over and over throughout the Scriptures.

God is not anything so much as He is Love. The most conspicuous statements in the Scriptures about our heavenly Father are the declarations concerning His love, His mercy, His compassion. There is no note that can be sounded concerning God's character that will so inspire faith as this one. In our revivals, I have seen faith rise "mountain high" when the truth of God's present love and compassion began to dawn upon the minds and hearts of the people. It is not what God *can* do, but what we know He *yearns* to do, that inspires faith.

By showing His compassion everywhere in the healing of the sick, Jesus unveiled the compassionate heart of God to the people, and the multitudes came to Him for help. Oh, how insidiously has Satan worked to hide this glorious fact from the people. He has broadcasted the unscriptural, illogical and worn-out statement, that the age of miracles is past, until he has almost succeeded in eclipsing the compassion of God from the eyes of the world. Modern theology magnifies the *power* of God more than it magnifies His *compassion*; His power more than it does the great fact that "the exceeding greatness of His power (is) to *usward*." But the Bible reverses this, and magnifies His willingness to use His power more than it does the power itself. In no place does the Bible say that "God is power," but it *does* say, that "God is *love*." It is not faith in God's *power* that secures His blessings, but faith in His *love* and in His *will*.

God's Love Veiled by Modern Theology

The first statement in our text above is, "the Lord is gracious," meaning, "He is disposed to show favors." This glorious fact, that shines with such brilliancy throughout the Scriptures, has been so eclipsed by modern theology that we hear everywhere, the Lord is *able* instead of "the Lord is *gracious*." Hundreds needing healing have come or written to us, saying, concerning their need of deliverance, "the Lord is able"; but their teachings, as well as their lack of teaching, has kept them from knowing that the Lord is *willing*. How much faith does it take to say "the Lord is able"? The *devil* knows God is able, and he knows He is willing; but he has kept the *people* from knowing the latter fact. Satan is willing we shall magnify the Lord's power, because he knows that this is not a sufficient basis for faith; but he knows the Lord's compassion and willingness is.

Before praying for the healing of people, we have to wait to teach them the Word of God until they can say, "the Lord is gracious," instead of "the Lord is willing." This is exactly what Jesus had to do before healing the leper who said, "If thou wilt thou canst." He showed His willingness, so that the man could really expect healing.

In the preceding sermon, we have presented many scriptural proofs of the Lord's present willingness to heal. But even when we can advance from saying "He is able" to saying "He is willing," this is not enough. The word "willing" is too tame to fully express God's merciful attitude toward us. "He *delighteth* in mercy" (Mic. 7:18). We have His attitude more fully expressed in II Chron. 16:9, "For the eyes of the Lord run to and fro throughout the whole earth, to show Himself strong in the behalf of them whose heart is perfect toward Him." This text exhibits our Lord as not only being *willing*, but *eager* to pour His blessings in great profusion upon all who make it possible for Him to do so. "For the eyes of the Lord run to and fro," or, in other words, He is ever hunting for opportunities to gratify His benevolent heart, because "He *delighteth* in mercy."

Benevolence is the great attribute of God; therefore, if you want to please Him remove the obstacles out of the way of the exercise of His benevolence. He is Infinitely Good, and He

exists forever in a state of entire consecration to pour forth
blessings upon His creatures whenever they make it possible,
which all may do. Suppose the vast Pacific ocean were
elevated high above us. Then conceive of its pressure into
every crevice to find an outlet through which it might pour
its ocean-tides over all the earth, and you have a picture of
God's benevolent attitude toward us.

A Serious Challenge

After being first properly enlightened, I challenge you,
Reader, to place yourself where God's mercy can reach you
without His having to violate the glorious principles of His
moral government, then wait and see if you don't experience
the most overwhelming demonstration of His love and mercy,
and the blessing will flow until you have reached the limit of
your expectation. Cornelius placed himself where God's
mercy could reach him by saying to Peter, "We are all here
present before God to hear all things that are commanded
thee of God," and he found God's goodness so great that He
could not wait for Peter to finish his sermon. Just as soon as
Peter had spoken enough to be a basis for their faith, down
came the blessing.

Not only is God *able,* but He is also *willing* to do "exceeding abundantly above all that we ask or think." His love is
so great that it could not be fully gratified by blessing all the
holy beings in the universe; therefore, it is extended to His
enemies "throughout the whole earth." It seems to me that
God would rather we should doubt His ability than His willingness. I would rather have a man who is in trouble say to
me, "Brother Bosworth, I know you would help me if you
could" (doubting my ability) than to say, "I know you can,
but I have no confidence in your disposition to help me."

Again, the text at the head of this sermon further states
that the Lord is "full of compassion; slow to anger, and of

great mercy." When I think of how the Lord so floods *our* hearts with His tender love, until, in intercession for others our hearts are too full of yearnings to utter their feelings (yearnings that "cannot be uttered"), I stand in awe, and wonder what *His* compassion must be. A mother's compassion for her suffering child makes her not only willing to relieve the child, but to suffer if she cannot. The Greek word *sumpathes*, (translated "compassion") means to suffer with another." Accordingly, Isaiah says: "In all their affliction He was afflicted." Is it not strange that this wondrous fact of His mercy toward the sick, so clearly seen and applied during the darker ages of the Old Testament, should be overlooked and set aside in this "better" age, in which is opened the way for the fullest possible manifestations of His mercy toward every phase of human need?

The Benevolent Heart of God Reaches All

Our text, after showing the greatness of His compassion, closes with the logical conclusion, "The Lord is good to *all*: and His tender mercies are over *all* His works." In other words, He is so "full of compassion" that he cannot be "a Respecter of persons" in the bestowal of His mercies. How could He (Who being unable to fully gratify His benevolent heart by blessing Holy Beings, extends His mercies to the wicked of earth) withhold the common blessing of healing from any of His own obedient children?

What a strange doctrine that the sick are not to look for as much mercy during this age of grace, which prophets and kings desired to see, and Angels desired to look into, as sufferers did during the darker ages. Is God now more willing to show the mercy of forgiveness to the devil's children than He is the mercy of healing to his own? The fact is, He loves

His own sick and suffering child even more than He loves the sinner, and "the mercy (compassion) of the Lord is from everlasting to everlasting (not upon sinners alone, but) upon *them that fear Him.*" "Like as a father pitieth *his* children, so the Lord pitieth them that fear Him." "As the Heaven is high above the earth, so great is His mercy toward them that fear Him," as well as to the sinner. The sick christian can say, with Solomon, ". . . there is no God like thee . . . which keepest covenant and showeth mercy *unto thy servants* that walk before thee with all their hearts" (II Chron. 6:14). Not some, but "*All* the paths of the Lord are *mercy* and truth (not unto His enemies, but) *unto such as keep His covenant* and His testimonies" (Psa. 25:10).

Instances of the Lord's Compassion

Now let us look at a few passages from the Gospels, showing the Lord's compassion.

> "And there came a leper to Him, beseeching Him, and kneeling down to Him, and saying unto Him, 'if thou wilt thou canst make me clean.' And Jesus, *moved with compassion* put forth His hand, and touched him, and saith unto him, 'I will; be thou clean.' And as soon as He had spoken, immediately the leprosy departed from him, and he was cleansed; . . . and they came to Him from every quarter" (Mark 1:40-45).

Here it was compassion that moved Christ to heal this leper.

> " . . . He departed thence by ship into a desert place apart: and when the people had heard thereof they followed Him on foot out of the cities. And Jesus went forth and saw a great multitude, and *was moved with compassion toward them, and* He healed their sick" (Matthew 14:13,14).

Here, as elsewhere, He was "plenteous in mercy" to "all that had need of healing"; and it was His compassion that moved Him.

> "And as they departed from Jericho, a great multitude followed Him. And, behold, two blind men sitting by the wayside, when they heard that Jesus passed by, cried out, saying, 'Have *mercy* on us, O Lord, thou Son of David.' And Jesus . . . said, 'What will ye that I shall do unto you?' They say unto Him, 'Lord, that our eyes may be opened.' So Jesus *had compassion* on them, and touched their eyes: and immediately their eyes received sight, and they followed Him" (Matthew 20:29-34).

Here these blind men asked for the mercy of having their eyes opened, and Jesus granted unto them the mercy of healing, proving that healing is a mercy as well as forgiveness. The sick, in those days, when seeking *healing*, asked for *mercy*. In our day most people think of mercy as applied only to the sinner, not knowing that His mercy is also extended to the sick.

God the Father of Mercies

Paul, who calls God the "Father of Mercies," proves it by healing all the sick on the island of Melita. Jesus said, "Blessed are the merciful (compassionate) for they shall obtain mercy." Job was healed when he prayed for his friends. According to one of the beatitudes, he obtained mercy by showing it. Referring to, and accounting for Job's healing, James 5:11 says, "The Lord is very pitiful, and of tender mercy," and follows with the direction to the Church, "is *any sick* among *you?* let him call for the elders of the Church," etc. In other words, because "the Lord is very pitiful and of tender mercy" let "any sick" in the Church today as well as Job obtain their healing also. Having provided all we need,

Jesus is still saying, as He did to the two blind men, "What will ye that I should do unto you?"

After Jesus had had compassion on the man in the tombs so possessed with a legion of demons that he cut himself with stones, and broke the chains with which they had often tried to bind him, when he was clothed and in his right mind he was so glad that he besought the Lord that he might remain with Him. "Howbeit Jesus suffered him not, but saith unto him, Go home to thy friends, and tell them how great things the Lord hath done for thee, and hath had *compassion* on thee. And he departed, and began to *publish* in Decapolis how great things Jesus had done for him: and all men did marvel" (Mark 5:19-20).

A Result of One Man's Testimony

And now let us read Matthew 15:30-31, and see the results of this one man's testimony, given to advertise the Lord's compassion. "And great multitudes (in Decapolis) came unto Him, having with them those that were lame, blind, dumb, maimed and many others, and cast them down at Jesus' feet; and He healed them: insomuch that the multitudes wondered when they saw the dumb to speak, the maimed to be whole, the lame to walk, and the blind to see: and *they glorified the God of Israel.*"

It was not their being sick, as some teach today, but their being healed, that caused these "great multitudes" to "glorify the God of Israel." Oh, how much glory would come to God, as well as blessings to the world, if every minister today would present clearly the Bible promises for healing to the sick, and then, as soon as each one was healed, he would, in his turn, publish the Lord's compassion throughout his "Decapolis." In a short time thousands upon thousands everywhere who are now sick would obtain faith in Christ for healing. It would then again be said of the *multitudes* that *they* "glorified the God of Israel." The higher critic and the modernist would soon be unpopular, and the false healing cults would not draw away from the Church the multitudes who are now being ensnared.

Not a Crime to Publish God's Goodness

It is stated above that this man "published" the Lord's compassion. Some oppose and write articles against us for publishing the testimonies of those who are miraculously healed. What is the matter? Is there anything wrong in obeying the Lord's command to "make known *His* deeds among the people?" Since Jesus died to open the way for His mercies to reach all the needs of man, we surely ought to be willing for them to know it. One would think to read some of the books and articles that are being written that it is a crime to let the people know about the Lord's compassion.

You will notice that in the Scriptures above quoted, as the result of miracles of healing His fame was spread abroad, "and *they came to Him from every quarter*." And "they followed Him on foot out of the cities," and "great multitudes came to Him." "Multitudes!" "Multitudes!" "Multitudes," everywhere.

It is the same today. Just as soon as it is known in any city that "this same Jesus" is actually healing the sick—as soon as the command is obeyed to "make known His deeds among the people," and His compassion is "published," the people come "from every quarter." I have never seen anything that would so break down all the barriers, and bring the people from every quarter, as the manifestation of the Lord's compassion in healing the sick. We have found, in our revivals, that as soon as the public find out what "this same Jesus" is doing, they come from the Methodist quarter, from the Bap-

tist quarter, from the Catholic quarter, from the Christian
Science quarter, from the Unity quarter, from the Spiritualist
quarter, from the Jewish quarter, from the poor man's quarter, from the rich man's quarter and from *every quarter*, and
multitudes hear the Gospel, and give their lives to God, who
would never even attend the meetings if there were no healing
miracles to reveal His compassion.

An Effect of Present-Day Healings

If Christ and His apostles could not draw the multitudes
without miracles, does He expect more from us? Instead of
the "ministry of healing" diverting from the more important
matter of salvation for the soul, we have seen more happy conversions in a single week than we ever saw in a whole year of
evangelistic work during the thirteen years before the Lord
led us to preach this part of the Gospel in a bolder and more
public way. As soon as our revivals get under way, hundreds
nightly crowd forward to give their hearts and lives to God,
and whole cities are put to talking about Jesus. Other
evangelists who have visited our revivals are now proving
this to be true in their own meetings.

In our last revival preceding the writing of this book, conducted in Ottawa, Canada, during the seven weeks of the
meeting, six thousand came for healing, and about twelve
thousand for salvation. I doubt if there would have been
more than one thousand for salvation had it not been for
the miracles of healing which displayed the compassion of
the Lord. The City and country were stirred as never before
in its history, and the largest crowds that ever gathered under
one roof for religious meetings in this capital of Canada,
filled the newly-built million-dollar Auditorium — the largest
building in the City. The attendance ran as high as ten
thousand in a single service, and on the jacket of this book

is a picture of one of these audiences. Before leaving the city, many hundreds of written testimonies were received from those healed or being healed from almost every kind of disease and affliction. To God be all the Glory!

Healing a Mighty Evangelistic Agency

One Baptist evangelist who, amongst other evangelists is now proving this to be true, has written, in one of ten pamphlets he has published on the subject, that healing is the greatest evangelizing agency that the Lord ever used, and that he would not return to the old way (new way) for all the money in America.

Now let us look at another passage concerning the Lord's compassion.

"And Jesus went about all the cities and villages, teaching in their synagogues, and preaching the Gospel of the Kingdom, and healing every sickness and every disease among the people. But when He saw the multitudes, He was *moved with compassion on them*, because they fainted, and were scattered abroad, as sheep having no shepherd. Then said He unto His Disciples, The harvest truly is plenteous, but the laborers are few; Pray ye *therefore* the Lord of the Harvest that He will send forth laborers into His harvest. And when He had called unto Him the twelve, He gave them power against unclean spirits to cast them out, and to heal all manner of sicknesses and all manner of disease . . . and commanded them, saying . . . Go, preach . . . heal the sick" (Matt. 9:35 to 10:8) .

Here, His compassion toward the sick is now becoming so well known that the "harvest" has become too great for the ONE REAPER. His compassionate heart is full of yearning over the increasing numbers who could not reach Him because of the press. "When He saw the multitudes, He was moved with compassion on them." It is as though He was able to personally minister to but a portion of them, and His compassion for the rest of the rapidly-growing multitudes is now moving Him to thrust forth other laborers to heal, as well as preach. *"His* harvest" is not only the same in character in our day, but it is also much greater than when He was here; and, because His compassion is still the same, He wants the same kind of reapers to reap the same harvest, or results, by preaching and healing in "all the cities and villages." His compassion manifested through these twelve new laborers soon necessitated the thrusting forth of seventy more, empowered to preach and to heal. Laborers of this kind are few today, while "the harvest" truly is plenteous beyond what it was then. What He was beginning "to do and to teach" is exactly what He wants done and taught everywhere. Instead of *ending* something, according to the modern idea, He was *starting* something, which He promised to continue and increase—not the twentieth century Gospel, but *"this* Gospel" (that He proclaimed) He said "shall be preached in all the world."

A Strange Reversal of Christ's Promise

Jesus, in John 14:12 and 13, emphatically taught and promised that the same mercy and compassion could reach the people through our prayers while He is our High Priest in Heaven. In fact, His departure was to open the way for His compassion to be manifested on a much larger scale. Isaiah prophesied of Him, "Therefore will He be exalted that He may have mercy . . . " Jesus said, "It is expedient (profitable) for you that I go away." This could not be true if His going away would withdraw, or even modify, the manifestation of His compassion in healing the sick. Is it not strange that many ministers today exactly reverse Christ's promise that the same and greater works shall be done by teaching that the age of miracles is past. Others do the same by teaching that God wants some of His devout children to remain sick for His glory; and many other traditional and unscriptural ideas.

Every man who teaches that healing is not for all who need it today, as it was in the past, is virtually teaching that Christ's compassion toward the sick has been at least modified since His exaltation. Worse yet, others teach that His compassion in healing the sick has been entirely withdrawn. To me, it is a mystery how any minister can take a position that veils and interferes with the manifestation of the greatest attribute of deity, God's compassion which is Divine Love in action. When Paul would make the strongest possible appeal for consecration, he said, "I beseech you by the *mercies* of God," which is the manifestation of His greatest attribute.

Two Important Questions

Jesus said, When He, the Spirit of Truth is come . . . He shall glorify Me." Could the Spirit glorify Christ to the sick by telling them that the age of miracles is past, or that Jesus, since His exaltation, has withdrawn or modified His ministry to the sick, after He, Himself, promising to do "*the* works . . . and greater works" during this age? Has the Spirit come to magnify Christ by modifying His ministry to His sick and suffering brethren while He is their High Priest, directly contrary to the glorifying of the God of Israel in Decapolis, occasioned by the healing of the multitudes? If so, then the not uncommon practice of praying for the sick to have fortitude and patience to bear their affliction instead of praying "the prayer of faith" for their healing, is right.

It is since He became our High Priest that He speaks from Heaven seven times, saying, "He that hath an ear, let him hear what the Spirit saith unto the churches." Men are say-

ing much today which the Spirit has *never* said, and which is
the opposite of what He *does* say. The following are a few
of the things the Spirit says for the purpose of glorifying
Christ.

> "Wherefore in all things it behooved Him to be made
> like unto His brethren, that He might be a merciful (com-
> passionate) and faithful *High Priest* . . . " (Heb. 2:17).

We have already shown that both the words "merciful"
and "compassionate" are given as the meaning of the Greek
adjective *eleemon* translated "merciful" in this passage. This
verse has no reference to Christ's compassion as manifested
during His earthly ministry; it refers only to His ministry
from Heaven, and to the fact that His incarnation was to
the end that He might show compassion as our High Priest
after His return to Heaven. "All that Jesus began to do
and to teach until the day He was taken up" is what, because of His unchanging compassion, He promised would
continue and be greater after He went away.

The Spirit further glorifies Christ by saying that He is
now "touched (Greek, *sumpatheo*—translated "have compassion," in Heb. 10:34) with the feeling of our infirmities,"
that He still "can have compassion" (Heb. 5:2); and that
He is "Jesus Christ, the same yesterday, today, and forever."
Let us worship Him, because His compassion is the same
today, and because as He looks upon all our infirmities He
is still "moved with compassion" and yearns to help us.

Of course, we recognize, and thank God, that many who
do not believe in Divine Healing *do* cooperate with the
Spirit in these glorious sentiments as pertaining to the more
important work of soul-saving; but how wonderful it would
be if all ministers and christians, instead of saying that
the age of miracles is past, would cooperate with the Spirit
by also proclaiming to sufferers these glorious sentiments

which the Spirit expresses while fulfilling His office-work of glorifying the exalted Christ. Instead of being priests and Levites passing by on the other side, the Church, in James 5, is commanded to be a "Good Samaritan," with compassion ministering to the physical needs of the sick and afflicted, binding up their wounds, pouring in the healing balm of wine and oil (the *Word* of God and the *Spirit* of God); for "He sendeth His Word and healeth them" by the power of the Spirit. Jesus pronounced a woe upon the Scribes and Pharisees for having omitted the weightier matters of *mercy* and faith.

In the fifth chapter of Acts we have another wonderful proof that Christ's compassion toward the sick is now the same; for we read, concerning the multitudes brought into the streets of Jerusalem, in the days after He had ascended to the Father, that "they were *healed every one*." Here it was, again, as our High Priest *in Heaven*, that Jesus did exactly what He did before going away. From Heaven He was "moved with compassion, and healed all who had need of healing."

Even in the last chapter of Acts, we find His compassion manifested from Heaven by the healing of all on the island of Melita. While He is our High Priest His compassion is so great that "He ever liveth to make intercession for us."

Again, His compassion for the sick, since He was glorified, moved Him to "set" (establish) in the Church the gifts of faith, of miracles and of healing for the recovery of the sick while He is our High Priest through the centuries. After Christ's exaltation, to express it in the words of Rev. W. C. Stevens, "We find, as a matter of course *and of necessity*, 'gifts of healing,' taking just such rank and prominence as they did in our Lord's personal ministry on earth."

Even Laymen May Pray for Sick

Again, it is His present compassion for the sick that caused Him, as our High Priest and Head of the Church, to command the elders, and even the laymen, to pray the prayer of faith for the healing of "any sick" during the Church Age (James 5:14). Rev. W. C. Stevens on this point remarks, "All preachers, teachers, writers and others who hand out the Word of Life to the people, should keep this direction (James 5:14) as continuously before the people as sickness itself constantly confronts them."

Even during His earthly ministry, our Adorable Lord would make any sacrifice, and suffer even the curse, itself, in order to open the way for His compassion to reach the most unworthy and the most provoking of His enemies. Both the bloody sweat of Gethsemane and the horrible tortures of Calvary were but the manifestations of His infinite compassion. He went to Calvary with "His face set like flint"; for, after He had been betrayed by the kiss of Judas into the hands of His crucifiers and Peter had cut off the ear of the servant of the High Priest, Jesus heals the ear of His enemy, and tells Peter to put up his sword; and He sheathed, as it were, His own sword, by holding in check the most natural impulse of His holy soul in refusing to pray when, by praying, He could have had, instantly, more than twelve legions of angels to enable Him to escape the agony of the cross. But, then, there would have been only a judgment seat, and no mercy seat, for fallen man with all his needs of body, soul, and spirit. In His substitutionary work for us He anticipated every possible need of Adam's race, and opened the way for mercy to reach every phase of human need. He was then, and is now, moved with compassion toward all who need His Presence as "Provider," "Peace," "Victory," "Shepherd," "Righteousness," and "Physician," which are the seven blessings secured by the tragedy of His Cross, and revealed to us by His Redemptive names. His Covenants, including the Covenant of Healing, are given because of His mercy, and "He keepeth covenant and mercy with all who love Him to a thousand generations" (Deut. 7:9).

How Not to Grieve the Heart of Jesus

. Doubting or ignoring His love and compassion grieves the heart of Jesus. It made Him weep over Jerusalem. So many times have ministers said, in these days, that we do not *need* miracles now, thinking of miracles only as signs to prove the Lord's deity, etc. I have said to them, "If you had a cancer eating your head off, *you* would need a miracle, would you not?" Most people today are so in the dark on this subject that it never occurs to them that there is mercy also for the sick. They never think of the gifts of healing and miracles as being the manifestation of Christ's compassion; and that, hour after hour, and day after day, for three years, He healed all who came to Him *because of His compassion.* Are not the needs of sufferers today the same as they were in that day? And do they not need as much compassion as ever in the past?

When we think of the countless numbers in despair, suffering with such intense agony that death would be a mercy, and to whom the physicians, after doing their best, have been obliged to say, "I can do no more for you," how precious it is to know that Christ's compassion, every moment, is still precisely as when it was manifested during the three years of His earthly ministry of love—a fact upon which we may absolutely rely.

We have shown that bodily healing is a *mercy* which Christ, Who was the expression of the Father's will, everywhere bestowed upon all who sought it; and we have the plain declarations, the "Lord is plenteous in *mercy* unto *all* (including the sick) that call upon Him" because His mercy "endureth forever"; and is "from everlasting to everlasting"; He is "full of mercy" "over *all* His works." Do not these Scriptures settle the matter? Instead of saying that the age of miracles is past, say, "It is written!" "It is written!"

5

How to Appropriate

The Redemptive and Covenant Blessing
of Bodily Healing

(NOTE—In this sermon we are repeating a few of the statements made in the previous pages, in order that this one sermon shall contain enough to lay a complete foundation for faith. This is done for the benefit of some who may need the prayer of faith for their healing before they have time to read the entire book).

The First Step

The first step toward being healed is the same as the first step toward salvation, or any other blessing that God promises; that is, for the sick person to know what the Bible clearly teaches, that it *is* God's will to heal until one has lived out the alloted span of life. Each individual sufferer must be convinced by the Word of God that his or her healing is the will of God; for it is impossible to have real faith for healing as long as there is the slightest doubt as to its being God's will.

It is impossible to boldly claim by faith a blessing which we are not certain that God offers, because the power of God can be claimed only where the *will of God* is known. For instance, it would be next to impossible to get a sinner to "believe unto righteousness" before you had fully convinced him that it was God's Will to save him. Faith begins where the will of God is known. Faith must rest on the will of God alone, not on our desires or wishes. Appropriating faith is not believing that God *can* but that He *will*. Those who claim to believe in healing, but say one word in favor of it and ten words against it, cannot produce faith for healing.

Faith Is Expecting God To Do

When God commands us to pray for the sick, He means us to pray with faith, which we could not do if we did not know His will in the matter. Until a person knows God's Will, they have no basis for faith, because faith is expecting God to do what we know it is His will to do. It is not hard, when we have faith, to get God to do His will.

When we know it is His will, it is not difficult for us to believe that He will do what we are sure He wants to do. It is in this way that every saved person has experienced the still greater miracle of the new birth. There can be no appropriation by faith until we are made to know by the Gospel what God has provided for us.

There is no doctrine more emphatically taught throughout the Word of God than that, through the Atonement of Christ, both salvation and bodily healing were provided, and that it is God's will to take away the sickness of His own, and to fulfil the number of their days according to His promise (Ex. 23:25 and 26). As the types in Leviticus 14 and 15 show that it was *invariably* through *Atonement* that sickness was healed, under the law of Moses, so Matthew 8:17 definitely states that Jesus healed all diseases on the ground of Atonement. This Scripture shows us that Christ's reason for making no exceptions while healing the sick who thronged Him was His Atonement, which He made for all Adam's race, including you. As multitude after multi-

tude pressed upon Him "to hear Him and to be healed
of their disesaes," it is repeatedly stated throughout the Gospels, "He healed them all." (Read Matthew 4:24; 12:15;
14:14; Luke 4:40; Acts 10:38). He could make no exceptions.
Why? Because in His coming Atonement "Himself took *our*
infirmities," etc. Since it is *"our"* infirmities He bore, it requires the healing of *all* to fulfil this prophecy. God carefully put this in such language that we would have to misquote it to leave ourselves out.

What Calvary provides is for all!

God's way of saving the soul, of healing the body, and of
doing everything else He wants to do, is to send His Word—
His promise—and then keep the promise wherever it produces faith. The Divine procedure in healing is stated in
the text, "He sendeth His Word and healeth them, and
delivereth them from their graves" (Psalms 107:20).

It is "the *Word* of God which effectually worketh" in
them that believe, and is "health to all their flesh" (See 1
Thess. 2:12; Prov. 4:22).

Just as a little girl's faith for a new dress comes by hearing the promise of her mother to buy it next Saturday, so
our faith for healing comes by hearing God's word, or
promise, to do it. Both the little girl's faith and ours "cometh by hearing." Now, the little girl could not, and would
not be expected to have faith for the new dress until her
mother promised it; so we cannot, nor are we expected to,
have faith for healing or salvation, or any other blessing,
until that faith comes by hearing the Word (promise) of
God to do it.

How could any one find "justification by faith" until it
was preached to him, and how could any one find healing
by faith until it was preached to him? It is the Scriptures
which are able to make men wise unto salvation. We must

see that the Creator and Redeemer of the body is also its Physician before we have reason to expect healing.

The Value of God's Redemptive Names

Now, since He heals us by sending His Word, what can be more His Word than His *Redemptive* and Covenant names, which were given, all seven of them, for the specific purpose of revealing to every man in Adam's race His redemptive attitude toward them.

When Christ commands us to "preach the Gospel to every creature," He means that we shall tell "the Good News" of Redemption. His seven *Redemptive* names reveal what our *Redemption* includes. He has many other names, but only seven *Redemptive* names; and these seven names are never used in the Scriptures except in His dealings with man. Not six names, not eight; but seven, the perfect number, because He is a perfect Saviour, His redemption covering the whole scope of human need. The blessings revealed by each of these names are all in the Atonement. For instance, Jehovah-Shammah means "the Lord is present," "made nigh by the blood of His cross."

Jehovah-Shalom is translated "the Lord is our Peace." This is in the Atonement because "the chastisement of our peace was upon Him."

Jehovah-Ra-ah is translated "the Lord is my Shepherd." He became our Shepherd by giving His life for the sheep.

So, you see, this privilege is in the Atonement.

Jehovah-Jireh means "the Lord will provide" an offering; Christ, Himself, being the Offering provided on Calvary.

He became Jehovah-Nissi, "The Lord our Banner," or Victor, by spoiling principalities and powers on the cross.

He bore our sins, and became Jehovah-Tsidkenu, "the Lord our Righteousness," opening the way for every sinner to receive the gift of righteousness.

Jehovah-Rapha is translated, "I am the Lord that healeth thee," or, "I am the Lord thy Physician." This, also, is in the Atonement; for "Himself took our infirmities and bare our sicknesses."

This completes the list of seven names, which were given for the purpose of revealing God's relationship toward us all under each of these seven titles. These seven names all belong abidingly to Christ, and it is under each of these seven titles that He "is the same yesterday, today, and forever." Jesus says to all who come to Him for any of these seven blessings, "He that cometh unto Me I will in no wise cast out."

This is the Good News that God wants preached to every creature, so that every creature may have the privilege of enjoying "the fulness of the blessing of the Gospel of Christ."

I say again, that nothing is more God's Word "settled in Heaven" than His redemptive name Jehovah-Rapha. No one has a right to change God's "I *Am*" Jehovah-Rapha to "I *Was*," because the "word of the Lord endureth forever."

Since Jehovah-Shalom, "The Lord our Peace," is one of Christ's redemptive names, has not every man a redemptive right to obtain peace from Him; and has not every man, likewise, a redemptive right to obtain victory from Jehovah-Nissi? Has not every man a redemptive right to obtain "the gift of righteousness" from Jehovah-Tsidkenu, etc.? If so, why has not every man a redemptive right to obtain healing from Jehovah-Rapha?

This Word (Jehovah-Rapha), was so accepted and believed by those to whom it was first sent that "there was not a feeble person among all their tribes"; and whenever this state of health was interfered with by their transgressions, as soon as they repented, typical atonements were made, and God was still Jehovah-Rapha *the healer;* not to some, but to all. God wants this name, as well as all others, to be sent "to every creature" with the promise "they shall recover," for "the Lord shall raise them up."

The Brazen Serpent a Type of Christ

God ratified this Word by the dying Israelites by sending them the added Word, "everyone that is bitten, when he looketh upon it (the type of Calvary) shall live." If bodily healing is not provided in the Atonement, why were these dying Israelites required to look at the type of the Atonement for bodily healing? As their curse was removed by the lifting up of the type of Christ, so ours is removed by the lifting up of Christ, the Antitype. Since the Spirit is given to us to make Christ real, why should we not look to Christ, Himself, with as much expectation as they did to the type?

It will be well to note that they could not look at the brass snake and their symptoms at the same time. Abraham's faith waxed strong while he looked unto the promise of God. Some people reverse this, and their faith waxes weak while they look at their symptoms, and forget the promise. Since God healed by sending His Word, which is the only basis for our faith, we will miss healing if we allow our symtoms to hinder us from expecting what His Word promises.

The Second Step

The second step is to be sure you are right with God, because our redemptive blessings are conditional. After we hear the Gospel, and know what it offers, Jesus says, "Repent and believe the Gospel." Only those who are right with God can follow these instructions. When seeking healing for our bodies there should be no compromise with the Adversary of our souls, because it is he who is the author of our diseases. Jesus may, but He has not promised to, destroy the works of the devil in our bodies while we are clinging to the work of the devil in our souls. It is hard to exercise faith for the removal of one part of the devil's work while we allow a worse part to remain. Until a man squarely faces and settles the question of obedience to God, he is not on believing ground. James says, "Confess your faults one to another . . . that ye may be healed." It is God's will "that thou mayest prosper and be in health even as thy soul prospereth." "If I regard iniquity in my heart the Lord will not hear me."

It is when our hearts condemn us not that we have confidence toward God.

The command for the sick to "send for the elders," was first written to Christians who had been *filled with the Spirit.* There is something wrong when a man desires the blessing but not the Blesser—His mercy but not *Himself.* It is not proper to seek His mercy while rejecting His Will. Do not ask for a little blessing while rejecting a big one. It is impossible to receive and reject Divine blessings at the same time.

God is waiting to say to Satan and disease what He said to Pharaoh, "Let My people go that they may *serve* Me" (Ex. 7:16). "Our first consideration, in all things, even in asking for the restoration of bodily health, should be the glory of God."—*Duffy.*

Strength for service to God is the only proper basis of approach when seeking health at His hand. The anointing with oil for healing is, itself, a symbol and sign of consecration.

We must desire our health for God's glory.

"What, then, does the anointing mean? Turn to Leviticus 8:10-12, and you get God's answer to the question. 'And Moses took the anointing oil, and anointed the tabernacle, and all that was therein, and sanctified them,' that is, he *set them apart for God.* The anointing 'with oil in the name of the Lord,' was an act of dedication and consecration, implying on the part of one anointed a full surrender to God of his hands to work for Him and for Him alone, of his feet to walk for Him and Him alone, his eyes to see, his lips to speak, his ears to hear for Him and Him alone, and his whole body to be the temple of the Holy Spirit."—Rev. R. A. Torrey.

"Beloved, I wish above all things that thou mayest prosper and be in health, *even as thy soul prospereth*" (III John, 2).

The Holy Spirit tells us to submit ourselves to God before He says "resist the devil," because no one can successfully resist the devil until he submits himself to God. When the devil is *thus* resisted he will not merely walk away; he will literally run—*"flee from you!"* (See Jas. 4:7).

The curse, including the different diseases catalogued in Deut. 28th chapter, came upon the people because their obedience and their service was not "with gladness and joyfulness of heart." The condition of heart that was responsible for the coming of those diseases mentioned in that chapter is not the condition for their removal. In other words, the condition of heart that was responsible for the curse in that day is not the condition of heart in which to come to Him for the removal of the curse in our day.

God's Promises Only to the Obedient

It is to those who will delight themselves in the Lord that He gives the desires of their heart. (See Psa. 37:4). God has not lowered the standard for the Day of Grace. It is only to the obedient—those who will "diligently hearken to the voice of the Lord" and "do that which is right in His sight" —that it is said, "The Lord will take away from *thee* all sickness." (See Deut. 7:15; Ex. 15:26).

> "Faith, you see, is the union of our hearts and wills with God's Will and purpose; and where this unity is lacking results are impossible. This is a *very important spiritual law,* to which, in our times, we have been woefully blind."—*Rev. P. Gavin Duffy.*

God says, of fearing the Lord and departing from evil. "*It* shall (itself) be health (Hebrew, medicine) to thy navel and marrow (Heb., moistening) to thy bones" (Prov.3:7,8).

Faith always implies obedience. Paul wrote to the Ephesians to obey the first commandment, "That it may be well with thee, and thou mayest live long on the earth" (Eph. 6:3). Naaman's surrender and obedience to the Word of God was complete before he was healed.

It is to those who "walk uprightly" that it is said, "No good thing will He withhold" (Psa. 84:11). Therefore, before seeking anything from God we should yield ourselves to the "first and great commandment," "Thou shalt love the Lord thy God with all thy heart . . ." for God says, "*Because* he hath set his love upon Me, *therefore* will I deliver him" (Psa. 91:14). He "keepeth covenant and mercy with *them that love Him* and keep His commandments to a thousand generations" (Deut. 7:9). *Therefore,* like the leper, let us come and *worship* Him when asking for healing.

"Length of days is in *her* (Wisdom's) right hand and in her left hand riches and honor" (Prov. 3:16). Marry her (Wisdom) and you get her possessions. Wisdom is here represented as a bountiful Queen, reaching forth blessings with both hands to all who will become subject to her government.

It is for "them whose heart is perfect toward Him" that "the eyes of the Lord run to and fro throughout the whole earth to show Himself strong." (See II Chron. 16:30).

"A sound heart is the *life of the flesh*: but envy the rottenness of the bones" (Prov. 14:30). An unsound heart is worse than an unsound stomach—a diseased soul worse than a diseased body. A disordered will is worse than a disordered liver. Paul said, "the body . . . for the Lord" before he said, "the Lord for the body."

The Bible teaches that the body is "bought with a price; therefore glorify God in your body, and in your spirit, *which are God's*" (I Cor. 6:20). "I beseech you, therefore, brethren, by the *mercies* of God, that ye present your bodies a living sacrifice . . . which is your reasonable service" (Rom. 12:1). Therefore present your body to Him if you want it healed. It is not until after it becomes His property that He promises to repair it.

First to the Cross for Cleansing

"The sure way for the sick is, first to the cross for cleansing, then to the Upper Room for the gift of the Spirit, then to the mount appointed for a life commission, and, lastly, to the Great Physician for strength for service." —*Bryant*.

"If the Spirit of Him that raised up Jesus from the dead dwell *in* you, He that raised up Christ from the dead shall also quicken your mortal bodies by His Spirit that dwelleth *in* you" (Rom. 8:11). In Christ; the True Vine, there is all the life for our souls and bodies that we need; but how are we to possess and enjoy this except by our *union* with the Vine. It is not apart from Him, but *"in Him"* that "ye are complete" (Col. 2:10).

Substitution without union is not sufficient for our possession and enjoyment of the life of the Vine. If you need

a miracle, get in tune with the Miracle-Worker. We enjoy
the Life of the Vine by our perfect union with the Vine.
Asking for healing while refusing to be led by the Spirit
is like asking a carpenter to repair the house while refusing
to let him in the house.

"As many as touched Him were made perfectly whole"
(Matt. 14:36). You cannot touch Him with a reservation;
therefore, like the woman who pressed through the throng
and touched Him, you must "elbow" out of your way, and
press beyond selfishness, disobedience, unconfessed sins,
luke-warmness, public opinion, traditions of men, articles
written against Divine healing; in fact, often press beyond
your own pastor, who may be unenlightened in this part
of the Gospel; press beyond doubts, double-mindedness,
symptoms, feelings and the lying Serpent.

The Holy Spirit, Who is sent to execute for us the blessings of redemption, is our Paraclete or Helper, and is ready
to help us press through and beyond all of these obstacles
to the place where we can touch Him for our needs. God
is waiting to pour out the Holy Spirit in fulness upon us,
Who comes as Christ's Executive to execute for us all the
blessings provided by Calvary, and pledged to us in His seven
redemptive and Covenant names.

It is still true that as many as touch Him are made whole.
How do we touch Him? By believing His promise. This
is an infallible way of touching Christ for anything He has
promised. We touch Him by asking, and believing that He
hears our prayers when we pray. When the woman touched
Him, it was her faith that made her whole; not a mere physical touch, for "the flesh profiteth nothing, the Spirit giveth life." Millions of sinners have *thus* touched Him for
the yet greater miracle of the new birth.

Not Mere Contact, But Union

As the sick touched Him and were made whole when Christ walked upon the earth, so, now, it is the privilege of all to actually touch Him, and the touch now unites us to Christ in a closer union than it did then. Not mere contact, but union as real as the branch and the vine. All that is in the Vine, including both spiritual and physical life, belongs to us — the branches.

The touch by faith can now bring us under the full control of the Holy Spirit, Who is the Miracle-Worker, as it could not do during Christ's earthly ministry, for "the Spirit was not yet given." Jesus is not less a Saviour and Healer since being glorified; He is *greater*. The privilege of touching Him now is much greater than when He was here in person, because more can now be received by the touch. From God's right hand He has more to give; therefore, He said, "It is expedient (profitable) for you that I go away." Since the Spirit comes to reveal Christ as He could not be revealed before He went away to send the Spirit, why cannot we approach Him for healing with at least as much faith as those who thronged Him in that day?

The foregoing shows the great importance of being right with God before asking for healing. The blessing of being right with God is a thousand times more desirable and enjoyable than the healing itself. I have seen the afflicted in body radiantly happy; but sinners in perfect health have been so unhappy as to commit suicide.

The Third Step

We will now endeavor to make plain how to *appropriate* healing. Getting things from God is like playing checkers, when, after one person moves, he has nothing to do until the other player moves. Each man moves in his own turn. So, when God has provided healing, or any other blessing, and sent us His Word, it is our move before He will move again. Our move is to expect what He promises *when* we pray, which will cause us to *act* our faith before we *see* the healing; because the healing comes in the next move, which is God's move.

God never moves out of His turn, but He always moves when it is His turn. When Noah was "warned of God *of things not seen as yet*," his move was to *believe* that the flood was coming, and *act his faith* by building the ship on dry land. So, when God says to "any sick," "the prayer of faith shall save the sick, and the Lord shall raise him up," you, like Noah, are informed of God "of things not seen as yet," and your move is the same as Noah's, which is, to believe and act accordingly. Fallen nature is governed by what it sees, by its senses, but faith is governed by the pure Word of God, and is nothing less than *expecting* God to do what He promises — treating Him like an honest Being.

By *expectation* I do not mean hope. One writer has well said, "We hope for what *may* be possible, but we expect what *must* be possible . . . with that expectancy that shuts out doubt or fear of failure, and shows unshakable confidence."

Faith never waits to *see* before it believes, because it "cometh by *hearing*" about "things not seen as yet," and "is the evidence of things not seen." All that a man of faith needs is to know that God has spoken. This imparts perfect certainty to the soul. "Thus saith the Lord" settles everything. "It is written" is all that faith needs.

Faith always blows the ram's horn *before*, not after, the walls are down. Faith never judges according to the sight of the eyes, because it is the evidence of things not seen but

promised. Faith rests on far more solid ground than the
evidence of the senses, and that is the Word of God which
"abideth forever." Our senses may deceive us, but God's
Word never!

When the little girl is promised a new dress next Saturday,
faith is the actual expectation which she has and manifests
between now and Saturday. When Saturday comes, and she
sees the new dress, faith for the new dress stops. Now, real
faith, always has corresponding actions. The little girl, because of her faith, claps her hands and says, "Goody! Goody!
I am going to have a new dress next Saturday!" and runs to
tell her playmates that she has the answer to her request.

God Cannot Lie

Jesus, at the grave of Lazarus, looked up, and said, "I
thank Thee, Father, that Thou *hast* heard me," though
Lazarus was still dead. The little girl is not afraid to testify
in advance that she is to have a new dress and when her
playmates say, "How do you know you are?" she confidently
replies, "Why! Mamma promised it!" Now, you have a better
reason for expecting healing than the little girl has for
expecting a new dress because the mother may die before
Saturday, but God cannot. The mother can lie, but God
cannot. The house may burn down with the mother's money.
Every case of faith in history was a well-grounded assurance,
produced by the promise of God alone, and acted upon before
there was anything visible to encourage the assurance, as
with the little girl "between now and Saturday."

Faith looks "not at the things that are seen." There was no
flood in sight when Noah built his ark. Stone walls had
never before fallen down at the blowing of rams' horns
and shouting. They were merely expecting what God promised, and when they acted their faith by blowing the rams'

horns while the walls were still up, this was *their* move. Then, of course, *God* moved in His turn, and down came the walls!

The whole eleventh chapter of Hebrews is written to show how each one who had faith acted "between now and Saturday."

God is so well pleased with the actings of faith that He has listed in detail many cases, as recorded in the eleventh of Hebrews.

"By faith, Noah" acted so-and-so. "By faith Jacob" acted so-and-so. "By faith Joseph" acted so-and-so. "By faith Moses" acted so-and-so. "By faith the walls of Jericho fell down." "By faith Abraham" acted so-and-so, when everything seemed contrary to what God had promised. It was by considering the *promise of God* (not her barrenness) that Sarah received strength to become a mother when she was past age.

These all acted with *nothing but the Word of God as their reason for expecting the thing He had promised.*

It is the same with every case of faith in history.

Jonah's symptoms were very real when he was inside the fish, and he did not deny them; but he called them "lying vanities." In other words, any symptoms that make us doubt the fact that "God is plenteous in mercy to *all* that call upon Him" should be regarded as "lying vanities." Jonah said, "They that observe lying vanities forsake their own mercy." Instead of listening to Satan and watching our symptoms, we must be "workers together" with God, Who heals by *sending His* Word and keeping it!

We must cooperate with Him by being occupied, not with what the devil says, but with *the Word He sends for our healing.*

Symptoms May Linger

Even when we do act our faith, symptoms do not always disappear instantly. After Hezekiah was healed, it was three days before he was strong enough to go up to the House of the Lord. In John 4:50-52, the nobleman, "believed the word that Jesus had spoken unto him," and when he met his servants he enquired of them the hour when his dying son "began to amend."

The Bible differentiates between the "gifts of healing" and the gift of "miracles." Christ could do no *miracle* in Nazareth because of their unbelief, but He healed a few sick ones. If every one were to be made perfectly whole instantly, there would be no place for the gifts of healing; it would be all miracles. Many people miss healing by trying to confine God to miracles. Christ's promise is that "they shall recover," but He does not say "instantly."

The symptoms of life in a tree remain for a time after the tree is cut down.

"Faith means we are confident of what we hope for, convinced of what we do not see" (Heb. 11:1 — Moffatt's translation). Convinced, of course, because God, Who cannot lie, has spoken. *How all-sufficient is this reason for believing!* Faith is, therefore, most rational. It is not, as many unthinking persons suppose, believing without evidence, but believing because of the very highest possible evidence, God's Word, which is "settled in Heaven." The Apostle James says, "I will show you by my actions what faith is." (Moffatt's translation). Faith therefore, is being so convinced of the absolute truth of the declarations of God which are recorded in the Bible that we act on them.

Faith Both Rational and Safe

What can be more rational, and what can be more safe and certain?

Faith is to receive the written promise of God as His direct message to us. His promise means the same as if He appeared and said to us, "I have heard your prayer." The Word of God is made life to our bodies in exactly the same way that it is made life to our souls, which is by believing His promise.

I have known some who had prayed for healing for as long as 40 years without receiving it; and then, as soon as they were told how to appropriate, the healing has come sometimes in a moment. We do not have to pray for 40 years, or for one week, for the blessing that Christ is eager to bestow. His compassionate heart yearns to heal us more than we have the capacity to desire it; but we keep Him waiting until we have the "faith that cometh by hearing" and act that faith, because God will not cheat and move out of His turn.

After seeing that Jesus bore our diseases as well as our sins on the cross, and therefore that we need not bear them, our next step is to appropriate by faith, which is the only scriptural way. The truth of the matter is, God gave us this part of our inheritance nearly 2,000 years ago and *He* is the waiting One — waiting for us to appropriate the blessing by faith. Two thousand years ago God "put away sin;" 2,000 years ago "God laid on Christ the iniquity of us all;" 2,000 years ago "Himself took our infirmities, and bare our sicknesses." God is the waiting party, waiting for us to be shown how to appropriate the blessing He has *already* given. II Peter 3:9. "The Lord is not slack (slow) concerning His promises . . . but He is longsuffering to usward." Or, as Weymouth translates, "The Lord is not slow in fulfilling His promises but He bears patiently with you." In other words, He is not slow concerning His promises, but *we* are *slow* and *He is patient* with us.

Most of us could have been saved five years earlier than we were. God was not making us wait, but we were making Him wait. It is the same with our healing.

When Ye Pray, Not Afterwards

Now, in Mark 11:24, Jesus tells us exactly how to appropriate any of the blessings purchased for us by His death. Having promised all that we need, He says, "What things soever ye desire *when ye pray;*" not after you pray 20 years; not after you get well; but while you are sick *when ye pray,* "believe that ye receive them and ye *shall* have them.

The condition of receiving what we ask God for is to believe that He answers our prayers when we pray, and that we "shall recover" according to His promise.

In other words, when you pray for healing, Christ authorizes you to consider your prayer answered, as when He stood at the grave of Lazarus and said, "I thank Thee, father, that thou *hast* heard Me," before He saw Lazarus come forth from the grave. When we ask for healing, Christ bids us say, with faith, "I thank Thee, Father, that Thou *hast* heard me," before we have yet seen the answer to our prayer.

When God's Word alone is our reason for believing that our prayer is answered, before we see or feel, this is faith!

"Jesus declared, "The *words* that I speak unto you *they* are Spirit and they are life." John says, "The Word is God." To receive the written words of Christ as the direct message to us is faith. This is the way the Word of God becomes life to us, both in our healing and in our salvation. For instance, the act of believing and receiving Christ according to John 1:12, is synonymous with the act of God which gives us, by His power, the new birth. By this same process also is Divine healing imparted to our bodies." (Writer not known).

Another has said, in substance, with the woman who touched His garment, faith, fact, feeling is the order of healing that God never departs from. If *we* depart from this order neither faith, fact, nor feeling will be as we desire, because they will not be as God desires.

I Thes. 2:13 says it is "The Word of God which effectually worketh also in you that believe." When His Word convinces us that our prayer is answered, before we have yet seen the answer, the Word begins to effectually work in us.

"God's Word never fails to work in those who accept it as such, because they are not entertaining doubts as to its being fulfilled in their own experiences . . . God has given all his blessings to Faith, He has none left to bestow upon unbelief."—*Harriet S. Bainbridge.*

When people say to me, "I do not know that it is God's Will to heal me," I ask them, "Is it God's Will to keep His promise?" If we are right with God, we should not consider ourselves any more than we would when men make promises to us. Not, Have I faith enough, but, Is He honest? It is not a question of how we feel, but what are the facts. Should the little girl get sick the next day, and feel badly, it has nothing to do with her mother buying her the new dress on Saturday. The Scriptures say, "If we ask anything according to His Will He heareth us." Is this true or not?

Does God answer prayer?

If you will steadfastly "believe that ye receive" (Mark 11:24) the answer to your prayer and act your faith, every one of you will be healed, though not always instantly.

God always moves after our move, which is the acting out of a "full assurance," produced alone by His promise before we see the answer to our prayer. Since healing is by faith, and "faith without works is dead," it is when we begin to *act* our faith that God begins to heal.

Our Faith Makes God Act

Our "work of faith" sets God to working.

Now, we cannot all act in the same way. As the ten lepers went they were healed. Jonah, when inside the fish, could not "went," but he did act his faith by saying, while still in the fish, "I will sacrifice with the voice of thanksgiving." And so, acting our faith by praising and thanking God in advance has been, throughout history, His appointed way for our appropriation of all His blessings. Hebrews 13:15 teaches us that our thank offering — our "sacrifice of praise" —is to be offered in advance for the blessing God has promised, and therefore we expect. Psalms 50:14, 15, says, "Offer unto God thanksgiving and pay thy vows unto the Most High, and call upon Me in the day of trouble: I will deliver thee, and thou shalt glorify Me."

Here, as elsewhere, we are required to offer thanksgiving while we are still in trouble, as Jonah did. Perhaps this was the very promise he claimed. "Let the needy praise thy name," that is, praise God in advance while you are still in need. "Let us come before His presence with thanksgiving" does not mean to get healed and then go from His presence thanking Him, but to come to Him with thanksgiving for healing before being healed. *"Enter* His gates with thanksgiving and into His courts with praise." We should go away with thanksgiving, but this is not faith.

Faith is what we have before we are healed. "They shall praise the Lord that *seek* Him." "Thou shalt call thy walls salvation, and thy gates praise." Without praise we are up against a solid wall with no gate; but when we begin praising, and appropriating, we hang our own gate, and walk through. "Be glad and rejoice for the Lord *will do* great things," and accordingly "they were continually in the Temple praising and blessing God," not after, but before they were filled with the Holy Spirit. It was "when they lifted up their voice and praised the Lord" that "the glory of the Lord filled the House of God." "They believed His *words* (not their symptoms, not the "father of lies") and sang His praises."

Make Satan Listen to Your Praises

Instead of your listening to the "Father of lies," make *him* listen to your praising God for His promise!

"Let everything that hath breath praise the Lord." The sick man has breath. In other words, while you are still sick praise Him because you are going to recover according to His promise. "Let not your heart be troubled." "In nothing be anxious (distracted), but with thanksgiving let your requests be made known unto God." "Casting all your care upon Him, for He careth for you."

Every sick Christian, while sick, has a thousand times more to be happy over than the most cheerful sinner in perfect health.

Praise God because "faith without works is dead." "In everything give thanks, for this is the will of God concerning you." "I will praise the Lord at *all* times, His praise shall continually be in my mouth." Since everything that hath breath is commanded to praise the Lord, the only scriptural excuse for not praising Him is to be out of breath. "By him, therefore, let us offer the sacrifice of praise to God continually, the fruit of our lips, giving thanks to His name." "Whoso offereth praise glorifieth Me." "Because Thy loving kindness *is better than life,* my lips shall praise thee." Praise Him "because it is a good thing to give thanks unto the Lord." "Give thanks at the remembrance of His holiness." Praise Him because to withhold praise will show either unbelief or ingratitude. Praise Him because "praise is comely for the upright." Praise Him because "God inhabits the praises of His people." Paul and Silas sang praises at midnight with their backs bleeding and their feet in the stocks, and God sang bass with an earthquake, which set them free.

Real faith rejoices in the promise of God as *if* it saw the deliverance, and was enjoying it.

With three great armies against Jehoshaphat, which, humanly speaking, would mean, annihilation, they praised the Lord "with a loud voice on high," when the only evidence that their prayer was answered was the naked Word of God; and *that* only through human lips. The next day, when they went out to the battle, and began to sing and praise, the Lord, in His turn, moved and set ambushments against the enemy, and the victory was won (II Chron. 20:18, 19). "We have also a more sure word of prophecy; for "holy men of old spake as they were moved by the Holy Ghost" (II Pet. 1:19-21).

"As in Eden the enemy succeeded in making void God's testimony as to the results of eating the forbidden fruit, so now he seeks to make void God's testimony as to the results of believing the Gospel. After God said, 'In the day thou eatest thereof thou shalt surely die,' the serpent said, 'Thou shalt not surely die,' and now, when God's Word plainly says, 'They shall lay hands on the sick and they *shall* recover,' the same serpent seeks to persuade them that they shall *not* recover. Is it rational to believe the 'father of lies' in preference to the Son of God, Who is Incarnate Truth? When coming to God for salvation or healing, it is essential for each one to decide whether he shall allow the hiss of the serpent to rise above the voice of God."

"Blessed are the ears that hear the pulses of the Divine whisper, and give no heed to the many whisperings of the world."—*Thos. a'Kempis.*

When, after you have been anointed for healing, Satan tells you that you will not recover, like Jesus, say to him, "It is written," "they *shall* recover;" "The Lord *shall* raise him up" (Jas. 5:14). Also, in this same passage, "in the Name of the Lord" means the same as if the Lord, Himself anointed you. Expect Him to honor His own ordinance and His own promise.

Why Listen to the Devil?

All the devil heard from the lips of Christ, when tempting Him, was, "It is written!" "It is written!" "It is written!" (Matt. 4:4, 7, 10). "Then the devil leaveth Him" (Matt. 4:11). But all we hear from some people is, "The devil says!" "The devil says!" "The devil says!" as though Christ's words were of less consequence than those of the devil! This was Christ's way; and it is the most successful way of resisting the devil. Let us not try another! "Neither give place to the devil" (Eph. 4:27). "Resist the devil and he will flee from you" (Jas. 4:7).

There is just one way of resisting the devil; and that is, by steadfastly believing and acting upon God's Word.

Whenever we are affected by any other voice more than the voice of God, we have forsaken the Lord's way for our healing.

What reason have you for doubting? You have no more reason for doubting than the sinner has when he repents and asks forgiveness of his sins. You have exactly the same reason for expecting to be healed that you had for expecting to be saved. "You have His Word for it, and if you cannot accept that to the point of acting upon it, then your faith is still very far from what it should be."—*Duffy*.

The Lord's Compassion a Basis for Faith

What a basis for faith is the Lord's compassion. Since Christ has redeemed us from sickness, surely His love and faithfulness may be trusted. The cross is a sure foundation and a perfect reason for the exercise of faith.

I do not recall who said, "Let us put our sickness away by faith, as we would put away sin. The consecrated Christian will not consciously tolerate sin for a moment, and yet how tolerant some are towards sickness. They will even pet and indulge their aches and pains, instead of resisting them as the words of the devil."

Harriet S. Bainbridge says, in substance, that the Lord Jesus has declared, concerning the sin, sorrow and physical misery of Adam's race "It is finished;" and has offered unto each one of us the gift of the Holy Spirit to enable us to realize and enjoy the great salvation He purchased for us. To believe without doubt that Christ's words "It is finished," is a literal statement of an unchangeable fact, invariably brings deliverance. The serpent is still denying this great saying of Christ to *our* great loss, just as he caused Eve to forget and disregard words which God had plainly spoken to *her*. It is by realizing that our redemption from sickness was actually accomplished in the body of our crucified Lord, and by whole-heartedly believing and receiving what God declares in His written Word about the matter, that the Holy Spirit gives us the personal experience of Christ as our Physician.

Present Day Results of Believing God

Following these instructions has brought soundness upon thousands who had before been taught that the age of miracles was past, and that God wanted people to remain sick for His glory, etc., etc. Those born blind are now seeing; deaf and dumb mutes from birth are now hearing and speaking; cripples from birth are now perfectly whole; epileptics for years are now free and rejoicing; many who were dying with cancers are now well, and praying the prayer of faith for the healing of others; and God is no respecter of persons. "If man will purge himself from these he shall be a vessel unto honor, sanctified, and meet for the Master's use, and thoroughly furnished unto every good work." This is never true while we are sick in bed. God's New Covenant provides that we each "shall be made perfect in every good work to do His will." This cannot be while we are sick, and this shows His willingness to make us well; in fact, His eagerness.

He cannot keep His Covenant with us without taking away our sicknesses and fulfilling the number of our days, according to His promise.

Since it is "by His stripes we are healed," let us not forget what our healing cost, but with gratitude and love, and consecrated service to God, let us stand on His promise and "blow the ram's horn" of faith and thanksgiving until the walls of our affliction fall down flat.

Faith does not wait for the walls to fall down; faith shouts them down!

6

Appropriating Faith

The Apostle Paul in his letter to the Galatians tells us exactly how God works miracles. "He (God) that ministereth to you the Spirit (the Spirit is the Miracle Worker), and worketh miracles among you, doeth He it by the works of the law, or by the hearing (message) of faith? Even as Abraham believed God" (Gal. 3:5). Moffatt translates this passage: "When He supplies you with the Spirit, and works miracles among you, is it because you do what the law commands, or because you believe the Gospel message? Why, it is as with Abraham, he had faith."

In this passage God tells us that He works miracles upon our bodies in exactly the same way as upon our souls, and that is, by having us hear and "believe the Gospel Message." In fact, God's way of doing everything is by making promises and then by fulfilling them wherever they produce faith. He says, it is with us "as with Abraham." How was it with Abraham? Note carefully:

He simply believed the word of God; "he had faith" that God would do exactly as He promised.

He was "fully persuaded" by the Word of God alone.

He held fast the beginning of his confidence when his faith was tested.

He was wholly occupied with the Word of God in the matter.

He refused to cast away his confidence when God, by telling him to offer Isaac, was apparently removing the visible encouragement to his faith.

He "considered not his own body" or the fact that he was about a hundred years old, neither "the deadness of Sarah's womb," as any barrier or any reason for doubting that Isaac would be born (Rom. 4:19). These things, which, according to nature, made the birth of Isaac impossible, were not considered by Abraham as the slightest reason for doubting. He knew his age; he recognized the barrenness of Sarah; he weighed the difficulties; but notwithstanding the impossible, he believed God.

"Under utterly hopeless circumstances," by "looking unto the promise of God" he "waxed strong in faith," being "fully persuaded" ("absolutely certain"—Weymouth) that God would fulfill His promise. Note well: it was by "looking unto the promise of God" that Abraham "waxed strong in faith." "Every one that looketh upon it" (God's remedy and God's promise) was likewise the condition God required for the healing of the dying Israelites (Num. 21:8). When coming to God for healing, be sure that this shall be your attitude, because there is no healing promised except on this condition.

To the extent that we base faith on our improvement, or are affected by our symptoms, or by what we see or feel, instead of by the word of God alone, just to that extent ours is not real faith. To be occupied with what we see or feel is to exactly reverse the condition God lays down for us to follow. "Every one that looketh at it shall live," simply means that every one who, like Abraham, so occupies himself with God's promise that he is no longer affected by symptoms, "shall recover." It means, the word of God (not what we see or feel) shall be the basis of our faith. Our "looking unto the promise of God is a good reason for looking to God for mercy, then there is no time to stop looking until God withdraws His word.

Note, it was by *continuing* to look unto the promise of God that Abraham experienced the miracle. To be occupied with symptoms and influenced by them, instead of God's word, is to question the veracity of God. Instead of making God a liar, Jonah, from within the fish, gave the name "lying vanities" to the symptoms and circumstances which seemed to stand in the way of his expecting God's mercy. Realizing that it was *symptoms* and not *God* that was lying to him, he said, "They that observe *lying vanities* forsake their own mercy." God never refuses mercy, but many "forsake" it by observing their symptoms, which are real, but which are "lying vanities," when they say to us that God is not "plenteous in mercy to all that call upon Him."

Abraham's faith was not based on anything he saw; and you must see to it that yours is not. All that Abraham could see was contrary to what he was expecting. After Isaac was born, Abraham had a prop for his faith that, through Isaac, "all the nations of the earth shall be blessed." With his eyes upon Isaac—the channel through which God was to fulfill the rest of His promise—it was easy to believe. So God tested his faith, telling him, by offering Isaac, to destroy the channel. This did not daunt Abraham. Real faith thrives on a test. Since he still had God's word for it, he was ready to remove every visible encouragement to his expectation and yet continue to be "fully persuaded." God had to halt him or he would have offered Isaac. This test was God's way of perfecting his faith not of destroying it.

If, after coming to God for healing, He finds you more encouraged by your improvement than by His Word, He may find it necessary to test your faith, in order to teach you the glorious lesson of believing His word, when every sense contradicts Him. Faith has to do only with the Word of God.

In Heb. 10:35, 36, God says, to all whose faith is based on His Word, "Cast not therefore away your confidence, which hath great recompense of reward, for ye have need of patience that, after ye have done the will of God, ye might receive the promise." "For we are made partakers . . . if we hold the beginning of our confidence steadfast to the end" (Heb. 3:14).

Directly contrary to this, after being anointed and prayed for, instead of rejoicing in the promise of God, I have heard some say in disappointment, "I thought sure I was going to be healed." Instantly, I knew they had never caught the idea of what faith is. Their idea was to get well first, and then to believe that God had heard prayer. If God's word were the sole reason for their expectation, they would have held fast the beginning of their confidence. It is never proper or reasonable to cast away your confidence as long as you have the word of God as its basis. It is promised that we shall be partakers, only on the condition that we "hold the beginning of our confidence steadfast." During the interim between God's promise and its fulfillment, instead of watching symptoms and casting away his confidence because he had nothing visible to encourage him, Abraham did exactly the reverse. By "looking unto the *promise* of God, he wavered not through unbelief; but waxed strong in faith, giving glory to God" (Rom. 4:20 R. V.). After Jonah, from within the fish, prayed for mercy, he did not cast away his confidence because there was no visible proof that his prayer was heard. He held fast his confidence, and added to it, in advance, "the sacrifice of thanksgiving." After marching around the walls of Jericho, Joshua and the children of Israel did not cast away their confidence because the walls of the City were still up. Their faith was based on God's word: "I have delivered Jericho into thy hands." If none of these cast away their confidence, why should you?

Your state of mind should be the same as Noah's, when he was building a ship on dry land and putting pitch into the cracks to keep the water out. In his mind, the fact of a coming flood was fully settled, and the word of God was the sole reason for this state of mind. Your state of mind should be the same as Abraham's. With him, the matter of Isaac being born was fully settled, even though all the symptoms were to the contrary. God's word, to you, concerning your healing, is just as clear and explicit as it was to Abraham.

In Mark 11:24, Jesus tells us exactly the conditions He requires for our appropriation of any of the blessings He has promised. He says, "What things soever ye desire, when ye pray, believe that ye receive them, and ye shall have them." That is, "ye shall have them" *after* you believe He has heard your prayer. As Jesus said, "I thank Thee that Thou *hast* heard me," while Lazarus was still dead; so we should be able to say, "I thank Thee that Thou hast heard me" while we are still sick. "Ye shall have them" is your answer from Jesus and is also your proof that your prayer has been heard. To faith, the *Word* of God is the *Voice* of God. He has not promised us that our healing shall begin until *after* we believe that he has heard our prayer. "If we ask anything according to his will, he heareth us." If this is true, then believe your prayer has been heard when you really pray. We must be able to say, "We know we have the petition we desire of him," not because we see the answer, but because "God is faithful who also will do it."

It is never proper to base faith on our improvement after prayer. I have heard some say, with great delight, "Oh, I am so much better since I was prayed for; now I know I will get well!" This means, that in the place of God's promise, they have some other reason for expecting to get well. *There is no reason for faith as good as the word of God.* Suppose, as soon as I pray for a man's healing, he could know he was just fifty per cent improved. This improvement in his condition is not near as good a reason for knowing he will entirely recover as is the promise of God, even though, after prayer, he should become fifty per cent worse. Suppose you promise your child a certain thing, and the next day you find that she is expecting exactly what you promised, but not because you promised it,—she has some other reason for expecting it. This would grieve you, for it would prove she did not trust your word.

It honors God to believe Him even while every sense contradicts Him! and He promises to honor those who honor Him. God has promised to respond only to the faith that is produced by and rests in His Word, or promise. Some expect to believe they have been heard as soon as they feel better. He did not say that He sent *better feelings* to produce faith and then healed them,—"He sent His *Word* and healed them." God Himself *"sent His Word,"* we did not *"worm"* it out of Him. How absurd, then, to doubt it. Is it not more rational to expect God to keep His promise than to expect Him to break it? Really, nothing can be more ridiculous or absurd than to allow symptoms or feelings to cause us to doubt the fulfillment of God's promises. Suppose your child, after being promised a new dress, should sprain her ankle, and should cast away her confidence for the dress because the ankle was painful. You say to her, "My dear child, I promised to get you the new dress. Can you not believe my word?" She answers: "But, Mother, my ankle still hurts. It doesn't feel a bit better; it seems to be getting worse." How absurd is such reasoning. Now if it be absurd to doubt one promise, because of pain, then it is equally ridiculous to doubt *any* promise. Suppose, again, that after you promise her the new dress, she runs to the mirror to see if she looks any more "dressed up," and then says: "I cannot see any difference; I do not look a bit better"; and then gives up the idea of having a new dress.

To learn how to believe that God hears us when we pray is a much greater blessing than is the healing itself, because then, the prayer of faith can be repeated ten thousand times, for ourselves and others, and thus our whole life be spent in obtaining the fulfillment of Divine promises.

Thus we have seen how Abraham experienced a miracle; and God says it is with us "as with Abraham." In this same way, therefore, we may all receive the fulfillment of God's promises, *"who also walk in the same steps of that faith of our Father Abraham"* (Rom. 4:12).

7

How to Receive Healing from Christ

In the case of the lifting up of the brazen serpent, a type
of the atonement which Christ adopted and applied to Himself, the condition to be met for the healing of the dying
Israelites is given in Numbers 21:8: "It shall come to pass,
that every one that is bitten, *when he looketh upon it* shall
live."

If, as some teach, healing is not provided by Christ's atonement, then why were these dying Israelites required to look
at the type of the *atonement* for bodily healing? And since
both forgiveness and healing came to them all by an expect-
ant look at the type of Calvary, why can not we all receive
as much from Christ—the Antitype? If we cannot, then the
type is placed in higher ground than Christ Himself, and
the type becomes a false prophecy.

"Every One That Looketh"

But notice that none were to receive healing except on
this condition: "Every one that *LOOKETH*."

LOOKING means, to be occupied and influenced with
what we are looking at. It is the equivalent of Abraham's
refusing to consider his own body and waxing strong in
faith by looking unto the promises of God. Being occupied
and influenced by our feelings or symptoms, is reversing the
conditions which God requires.

LOOKING means *attention*. After God gave the Covenant of Healing and revealed Himself as our Healer by the

redemptive name Jehovah-Rapha, the condition He laid down was that they should *"Hearken diligently and do all."* This means *attention* and *heed* to His Word. Jesus, in Mark 4:24, also taught us that it is by our *attention* and *heed* to God's Word that we measure to ourselves His blessings. "The Word of God is the seed" which, like all seed, when it is put into good ground, has the power to do its own work. And attention and heed to the Word of God is the way to get it into "good ground" and to keep it there.

Satan cannot hinder the "seed" from doing its work unless we allow him to get the seed out of the ground. He can only do this by getting you to turn your attention away from the Word of God to your symptoms. Jonah called his symptoms "lying vanities" and said, while still in the great fish, "I will *LOOK* again toward Thy holy temple," and then we hear him offering "the sacrifice of thanksgiving." This shows what *LOOKING* means.

LOOKING also means *expectation.* To look unto God for salvation means to *expect* salvation from Him. He says to us all: *"Look* unto Me, all ye ends of the earth, and be ye saved." Since God has provided and promised healing, we should dismiss from our minds the slightest thought of failing to be healed.

The word *"LOOKETH"* is also translated *"CONSIDER."* And we read that Sarah *"considered* that she could rely upon Him who had promised." Instead of considering her age, she received faith by considering the Word of God.

The word *"LOOKETH"* is in the continuous present tense. It is not a mere *glance,* but a continuous "stare" until you are well. It was a *"steadfast* faith" that brought the fulfilment of God's promise to Abraham. The healing process goes on while we are *looking* unto the promise. We are to think faith, speak faith, act faith, and keep it until the promise is fulfilled. By being occupied with symptoms or feelings, we violate the conditions and thereby turn off the switch to His power.

The Sight of Faith

We read in Heb. 11:23-27, that Moses "endured as [by] *seeing Him who is invisible."* As far as the optic nerve is concerned, "faith is the evidence of things *not seen."* But as far as the enlightened "eyes of our understanding" are concerned, faith *is* the evidence *of things seen*. Walking by *faith* is walking by *sight* of a better kind. We are to spend our lives *looking* at far better things than can be seen with the optic nerve. We see with the eye of faith the glorious things that are invisible to the natural eye. After all, it is the mind and not the optic nerve that sees. You cannot see your money in the bank except with your mind. When you draw a check, it is by faith in what you *see,* not with your eyes, but with your mind.

Faith is the most rational thing in the world, because it is based on the greatest of facts and realities. It sees God; it sees Calvary where disease and sin were canceled. It sees the promises of God and His faithfulness, which are more certain than the foundations of a mountain. Faith sees the health and strength given on the cross as already belonging to us; it receives the words: "Himself took our infirmities, and bare our sicknesses," and acts accordingly. What the eye of faith sees, the *hand* of faith appropriates, saying, "This is mine by virtue of the promise of God." Faith refuses to see anything but God and what He says.

Faith's Glorious Realities

It is a great mistake to suppose a thing is not real because it can not be seen with natural eyes. Suppose you should trust me to blind-fold your eyes and to lead you down the

street. The pavement under your feet is just as real as though
you could see it. Every time you take a step you are acting
a faith which "is the evidence of things not seen" by natural
eyes. You see only with your *mind* what I see with my eyes
and describe to you. The great spiritual realities and facts
which God sees and tells us about are just as real as though
we could see them with natural eyes. Because of God, His
faithfulness, and His promises, faith is the surest ground
that it is possible to stand on. To the man who is not enlightened or who does not see the promise of God, it is
stepping out into space; but to those who have faith in God's
Word, it is walking on the foundations of the universe. By
merely standing on the naked Word of God, millions of sinners have been "translated out of the kingdom of darkness
into the kingdom of God's dear Son." Millions have also been
taken from this world to heaven. The promise of God has
been better to them than a stone ladder reaching from this
world to heaven which could be seen with natural eyes.

Jesus tells us that He came "that they that see not [with the
natural eye] might see" with the eye of faith. After ascend-
ing to heaven, where He could no longer be seen with the
natural eye, He counselled us to anoint our [spiritual] eyes
with eyesalve that we might see. By doing this, Peter was
made to rejoice more over what he saw with his new sight
than he ever had over what he saw with the optic nerve.
Walking by this better kind of sight is the happiest life possible on earth because of the superiority of what we are constantly beholding—the best things—the joy-producing realities. Supernatural joy is always the result of using our better
pair of eyes.

It is important to see that real faith is occupied with God's
power and mercy, not with human weakness. God invites
us to take hold of His strength. He says: "To them that have

no might He increaseth strength." He says also: "Let the weak say, I am strong." It is as we obey Him and do this, believing, *on the authority of His Word,* that we have His strength, even when we *feel* weak; that "His strength is made perfect in [our] weakness." We must believe what God says in spite of how we feel. One reason

Why Some Fail to Receive Healing

is because they believe what their five senses tell them in the place of believing the Word of God. We should realize that the five senses belong to the *natural* man and that they were given to us to be used for the things of this world. But the things of God cannot be discerned, appropriated and known by the *natural* senses.

No kind of physical sensation, such as pain, weakness or sickness, can ever be a good reason for doubting the fulfillment of any Divine promise. How foolish it would be for me to doubt the promise of Christ's second coming because I felt sick or weak, or had a pain. And if a pain is not a good reason for doubting *one* promise, it is not a good reason for doubting *any* promise. God is just as faithful to one promise as to another. Therefore it is equally as foolish to doubt God's promise to heal because of pain or any disagreeable feeling, as it is to question Christ's second coming because of these things.

The ground upon which we claim the forgiveness of sins is the fact that Christ bore them "in His own body on the tree" (1 Peter 2:24), and we must believe that we are forgiven *before* our feelings can be any different. It is in exactly the same way and on the same ground that we are to appropriate *physical* healing from The Great Physician." The healing of both our souls and bodies is based on the unchangeable truth of Christ's finished work, not on our feelings.

When God gives you the Redemptive name, "Jehovah-Rapha," thereby saying unto you, "I am the Lord that healeth thee," He wants you to answer with faith, *"Yes, Lord, Thou art the Lord that healeth me."* He wants exactly what He says to be true in your experience, and you can make no mistake in saying and steadfastly believing what He says—that He at the present moment is actually healing you and will continue working until you are "perfectly whole." Faith is saying and believing what God says and acting accordingly. The blessings we take by a steadfast faith in God's promises will always materialize.

We Must Not Be Double-Minded

When appropriating the healing Christ has provided, we MUST NOT BE DOUBLE-MINDED. James says: "But let him ask in faith, nothing wavering. For he that wavereth is like a wave of the sea driven with the wind and tossed. For let not that man think that he shall receive anything of the Lord" (James 1:6, 7). We must, as it were, behead ourselves and put on "the mind of Christ"; which means to see only what He says and to act accordingly. This is implied in our asking "IN FAITH." Paul tells us to "put off the old man with his deeds," and this includes the old man's habit of thinking only according to the evidence of the five senses. Putting on the new man and having the mind of Christ, includes our thinking and believing what is written, and saying, as He did, "It is written." Remember the "new man" is not governed by the evidence of the senses.

The Word of God Is Powerful

The Bible tells us there is no word of God without power. Psalm 120:7 tells us: "He sent His Word and healed them."

This is His way of healing both our souls and our bodies. I have known of a number being healed after reading the words in Isaiah 53:5, "By whose stripes we *ARE* healed," and by then saying, "God says I am healed, and I am going to believe God and not my feelings." By saying and repeating what *He* says and acting accordingly even cancers have disappeared. When we steadfastly believe and act our faith in God's Word, nothing can keep the power in the Word from making all things to become exactly as the Word says. All we have to do is firmly believe what the Word says and resolutely refuse to see, believe or think of the things that contradict the Word. We are to take sides with God and believe that all we need for spirit, soul and body is ALREADY OURS. God said to Abraham: "I *HAVE made* thee the father of a multitude," and by taking the new name "Abraham" which means "the father of a multitude" the patriarch in faith continually repeated God's words after Him: "I *AM* the father of a multitude," and by thus counting the things that are not as though they were, and giving glory to God in advance, exactly what God said became true.

"As you believe that God has done and given, all He says He has done and given, and as you constantly obey His Word, God makes all the old things leave you and makes all that is of Christ appear in you" (Mrs. C. Nuzum).

"2 Peter 1:3 tells us that

God Has Already Given Us All Things

that pertain to life and godliness. This includes all we need for spirit, soul and body, for this life and for the life to come. Jesus purchased all this for us, and God tells us He *has already* given it to us. Isaiah 53:5 and 1 Peter 2:24 tell us that God *has* healed us. Col. 1:13 says God *has* delivered us from the power of darkness. In Luke 10:19 Jesus said:

'Behold, I give you power over all the power of the enemy: and nothing shall by any means hurt you." Romans 6:18 tells us that we are free.

"When appropriating all this, God warns us, in the case of Peter, to never look at our circumstances and feelings. The waves were just as high when Peter walked perfectly on the water as when he sank. While he did not look at them, they could not hinder him; but the minute he looked at them, he doubted and went down. The wind also was just as great when Peter walked perfectly, as when he sank. When he did not pay any attention to it, it could not hinder him. God here teaches us that if we are occupied with looking and feeling, instead of with Him and His Word, we will lose all He offers us. On the other hand, by steadfastly refusing to see anything but God and what He says, we shall have and keep everything that He says He has given us" (Mrs. C. Nuzum).

"Hold Fast That Thou Hast"

"Satan is busy trying to take from us what we take from God, and so God bids us, 'Hold fast that thou hast' (Rev. 3:11). Jesus gave Peter power to walk on the water, but the devil took it from him by getting him to fix his attention on the wind (representing things we feel), and on the waves (representing things we see). Peter had the power, and used it; but lost it by doubting" (Mrs. C. Nuzum).

How many lose the manifestation of healing already in operation, by turning their attention from Christ and the Word of God to their feelings. Before taking the step of faith for healing, get this matter fully settled, that after taking the step, you are going to see nothing but God and what He says. From that moment doubt should be regarded as out of the question and out of reason, because the evidence upon which you have planted your feet is the Word of God. To watch your feelings or symptoms would be like a farmer digging up his seed to see if it is growing. This would kill the seed at the root. When the true farmer gets his seed into the ground, he says with satisfaction, "I am glad that is *settled*"; and he believes that the seed has begun its work before he sees it grow. Why not the same faith in the "Imperishable Seed," the Word of God, and believe that it is already doing its work without waiting to see?

In receiving supernatural healing, the first thing to learn is to cease to be anxious about the condition of the body; because you have committed it to the Lord and He has taken the responsibility of your healing. You are to be happy and restful in the matter because you know from His own Word that He takes the responsibility of every case committed to Him. When receiving healing by faith, the body and its sensations are lost sight of and only the Lord and His promises are in view. Before being conscious of any physical change, faith rejoices and says, "It is written." Jesus won His great victories by saying, "It is written," and believing what was written. Any unfavorable feeling should be regarded as a warning not to consider the body, but to consider all the more the Lord's promise and to be occupied with Him. How much better to be in communion with God and rejoicing in His faithfulness, than to be occupied with a sick body. In this way we have seen multitudes make great spiritual advancement, while others have forfeited sweet communion with God by being occupied with their feelings and symptoms.

How Faith May Be Perfected

In Mark 9:24, we read that the father seeking healing for his child, "cried out, and said with tears, Lord, I believe;

help Thou mine unbelief." By asking Christ to help him, he received the needed help, thereby rising to a place of power above the apostles and succeeding where they had failed. In the Greek the Holy Spirit is called *"The Paraklete,"* which means "Helper." Thank God! the Christian can always have His help whenever it is needed. The Holy Spirit is always ready to work in us "that which is well-pleasing in His sight"; and this in a special sense includes *faith,* because "without faith it is impossible to please God." Since faith is especially pleasing in His sight, He wants to produce it in our hearts by His Word and by His Spirit. The Holy Spirit is always ready to help every Christian to exercise faith for any blessing God has promised them in His Word. The Bible tells us that Christ is able to save us to the uttermost, and this includes particularly His saving us from our unbelief, which is the sin of which the Holy Spirit came to convict us. Therefore, with a resolute purpose to hearken only to His Word, confess to God your unbelief and count on Him for deliverance from it, the same as from any other sin. His grace is always sufficient to cause faith to triumph for the appropriation of any mercy He has provided. The Holy Spirit is always ready to execute for us the fulfillment of any promise God has given.

What Constitutes a Man Righteous?

What is it that constitutes a man righteous? Over and over again we are told that Abraham was ACCOUNTED RIGHTEOUS. Very simple is the story as to *how his righteousness was determined.* HE BELIEVED GOD AND ACTED ACCORDINGLY. He so believed and acted as to receive from God the fulfillment of His promise. To do this, is the sum-total of righteousness. Nothing can ever be so important, and such a privilege, as this, because it is in this way alone, that

God's glorious program for the individual and for the Church can be carried out. In no other way can the will and work of God be done by anyone. When Christ was asked the question, "What shall we do that we might work the works of God?" His answer was, "This is the work of God, that ye believe . . . " It is only where he finds the exercise of living faith for the fulfillment of His promises that God can work. Since it is by thus believing God that we are accounted righteous, it is *unbelief* that constitutes us unrighteous. Unbelief is wicked and unrighteous because it hinders and sets aside the Divine program which consists of all that God has promised to do in response to faith. No wonder that it was the sin of unbelief of which God sent the Spirit to convict the world. Anything short of our having a living faith for the will and work of God to be done, even though we may call it religion, is something else in the place of His righteousness, and therefore it is unrighteous. Christ's ability to save us unto the uttermost consists in His ability to save us from our unbelief, which is so deadly to the glorious Divine program. The Holy Spirit is given to guide us into all truth so that we might believe it, in order that the whole program of God may be carried out. How many there are who believe *IN* God, but who do not believe *GOD* as Abraham did. A steadfast faith for what God has revealed to be His will for us, is our whole duty and from every standpoint our greatest privilege. How God would sweep the world with His mighty power if all who profess His name were to set out to discover all Divine Truth, to believe it with an appropriating faith and to act accordingly!

Faith in God has a much stronger foundation and a much stronger "HELPER" (the Holy Spirit) than either doubt or sin or disease has. The Holy Spirit will free your mind of all doubt if you will rely upon Him to do it, and if you will keep your attention on the Word of God.

The glorious, and lasting realities which God has provided for the eye of faith to behold, when really and steadfastly beheld, *always* becomes stronger than the cancer or the disease which the optic nerve sees. Doubt and sin and disease can *always* be destroyed by the right use of the "eyes of our understanding." This is the infallible method for our appropriation of all of God's blessings. All the glorious victories of faith recorded in the eleventh chapter of Hebrews, were the result of the proper and persistent use of their better sight.

"The law of the Spirit of life" which heals our souls and bodies, is much stronger than "the law of sin and death." This law, when not hindered by us, will win every time in a million. Every one who sets himself to obtain the benefits of the atonement, has an infinitely capable "HELPER" whose power, when relied upon, can never fail. As God's *grace* is stronger than sin, *so is Christ's healing virtue much more powerful than the strength of any disease*. And the evidence God gives us for faith, (His own Word) when it occupies the mind is much stronger than any evidence Satan can give us to make us doubt.

What Is the Exercise of Faith?

Jesus said to the man with the withered hand, "Stretch forth thy hand." Christ first gives faith, then calls it to its wondrous exercise. The man stretched forth his hand in reliance upon Divine strength, and it was made whole. As we put forth effort in reliance upon God, to do what without Him is impossible, God meets us with Divine power, and the thing is done independent of nature. Concerning anything that God calls us to do, "All things are possible [not

to him that feels able in himself, but] to him that *believeth*."
We see this man's ability not in himself, but *in Christ*, in
whom every part of salvation is contained. "I can do *all*
things *through Christ* which strengtheneth me." Through
our union with Christ, the True Vine, the strength is *already* ours, but must be put to use. It was the effort to put
forth his hand which opened the way for the healing touch
to be given and the divine life to flow. This *act* of faith,
begun in the natural, became a way of entrance for the supernatural to meet the man's need. It led at once to an action
wholly supernatural, by virtue of the Divine power imparted
—to an exercise of the body not possible according to former
conditions—an act independent of natural forces and wholly
dependent upon God.

The act of faith is not only a *physical* act, it includes the
exercise of the *heart* and *mind* toward God. The full exercise of faith means that we think faith, speak faith, act faith.
This brings the manifestation of all that faith takes according
to the promise of the Word. You may be asking, "How can
one exercise faith for the healing of blindness or of an affliction which does not interfere with the motion of the body?"
To the blind man Jesus said: "Go wash in the pool of Siloam." This act gave the man an opportunity to exercise
faith in heart, mind and body. It was the same with Naaman,
with the ten lepers, and with the centurion. In each case
they went relying upon the Word of Christ and believing
the healing was theirs before it was manifested to sight.

Should you deposit a thousand dollars in the bank and
come and tell me that you had made me a present of that
amount, if I believed you, I would act my faith and draw
checks on the bank as I needed the money. I have not seen
the money in the bank, but it is just as much mine as though
I saw it and had it in my hands. Just so healing for our

souls and bodies is in Christ, Whom God has made the treasury of all He is. Sickness, from which I have been redeemed, does not belong to me, but healing does. Therefore, I begin to check on healing. How? By attempting in His name what I cannot do without Him. This is acting faith; checking health and strength from the Bank of God. It is counting on something we do not see or feel, but which we know from God's own Word is ours, in the same way that the money in the bank is ours, although we do not see or feel it.

The Girdled Tree

"Some one may ask: 'How can I say that I am healed, when I see disease in the body and am conscious of pain?' There is an illustration in nature sometimes given which makes the truth clearer. One method of killing a tree is to girdle it, and when we see a tree girdled we think of it as a dead tree. Still its foliage is fresh and green for a while and gives evidence of life. The natural eye sees life. The mind's eye, which has knowledge beyond what nature beholds, sees death. In time the leaves wither and fall, and death, which the mind's eye saw from the first, becomes manifest to the senses. So it is when we take healing for the body. As we claim the *Word* of promise, in faith receiving a finished work, the 'sword of the Spirit' strikes the death blow to disease. For a little time symptoms may remain; but the eye of faith which beholds the Crucified One sees disease cancelled and health given, and, 'calling the things which be not as though they were,' the new life is manifested in the body. That which the eye of faith saw from the first as the truth becomes manifest to the senses. Faith sees God in His love and omnipotence making good the word" (From "Gems of Truth on Divine Healing").

Being governed by natural sight is unscientific because it does not take into account all the facts. It overlooks the greatest and best of facts. Healing by natural means only is unscientific because it overlooks important facts—the supernatural agency in disease as well as the privilege of the supernatural in its recovery.

We thank God for the thousands who have made great spiritual advancement while receiving healing in this way. The process of faith which brings the healing is a far greater blessing than the healing itself. Many throughout the Scriptures became famous for faith as a result of seeking God for what we call *temporal* blessings. When we have learned the process of faith for receiving healing, we have learned how to receive everything else God promises us in His Word. The Church could win millions for the service of God, and make them fighters of "the good fight of faith," by offering to them the healing of Christ purchased for them. May you, dear reader, by learning to be healed in this way, advance into a life of faith and usefulness in the kingdom of God.

8

How to Have Your Prayers Answered

"The Past Tenses of God's Word"

It is important for seekers after the mercies of God to see that appropriating faith is *taking* and *using* what God offers to us. *Hope* is *expecting* a blessing some time in the *future;* but *faith* is *taking now* what God offers.

We are to believe what God says He has done for us and act upon it — taking our blood-bought liberty just as the slaves of the south did after the "Emancipation Proclamation" by Abraham Lincoln.

"The Gospel is a world-wide emancipation proclamation of liberty from service and bondage to the old tyrant master of sin and sickness — the devil." When Jesus said "It is finished" He meant that the work was done—completed as God sees it; and God expects us to reckon as done what Jesus says was done. The past tenses of God's word mean a settled, sealed, and final decision of His Will.

In Galatians 3:13, we read "Christ *hath* (past tense) redeemed us from the curse of the law, being made a curse for us." God has put our redemption from the curse of the law in the past tense, and we receive our deliverance when we do the same. In Deut. 28th chapter, we see that the curse of the law includes all diseases.

In God's Word we read "Surely He *hath* (past tense) born our sicknesses and carried our pain" — "Himself *took* (past tense) our infirmities and bare our sicknesses" — "By Whose stripes ye *were* healed."

God wants us all to appropriate the past tenses of His Word regarding His redemption of our souls and bodies from sickness and disease and go forth in obedience acting as if we believed Him. When God puts a promise in the past tense, He thus authorizes and expects us to do the same. Nothing short of this is appropriating faith.

In Mark 11:24 Jesus authorizes us and commands us to put the reception of the blessing we pray for in the past tense. He says, *when we ask* for what He offers, "Believe that ye *have received* them, and ye *shall* have them." We are to continue to believe that God gave us what we asked for when we prayed, and continue to praise and thank Him for what He has given us. It is *after* we believe we have received what we ask for — after we believe He has heard our prayer, that God goes to work. *Then* the imperishable seed — His Word, begins to grow.

The farmer has to get the sowing of his seed into the past tense before it is possible to reap a harvest; and the permanent receiving of God's Word — the "imperishable seed" into the "good ground" of our heart, thus getting it into the past tense, is necessary before the seed *can* begin its work.

Believing that God has already heard our prayer before the blessing is manifested, is the soil in which the "imperishable seed" — (His Word) grows and bears fruit. Believing that God *has* heard our prayer gets the seed into the ground, and *then,* (and not before) it goes to work.

Jesus, at the grave of Lazarus, said, *while Lazarus was still dead,* "I thank Thee that Thou hast heard me." The sick who pray for healing are to say before the healing materializes, "Father, I thank Thee that Thou *hast* heard me." The Prayer of *faith* is believing our prayer is heard *before* the answer materializes — before the answer is manifested. "This is the confidence that we have in Him, that, if we ask anything according to His will, He heareth us: And if we know that He hears us, whatsoever we ask, we *know* that we *have* the petition that we desire of Him."

It is *before* having experienced or being conscious of any change whatsoever that faith rejoices and says "It is written." When we ask for healing we are to say on the authority of God's Word, "I thank Thee that Thou hast heard me."

Faith refuses to see (as reason for doubting) anything contrary to the Word of God. It sees the health and strength bequeathed to us as already belonging to us because of the death of the Testator. By His death the will is in force. Jesus says to us, "As thou *hast* believed (past tense), *so* be it unto thee."

With our natural eyes we see only the temporal and inferior things of earth, but with the enlightened eyes of our understanding we behold the superior, satisfying and lasting realities of God's spiritual and eternal Kingdom.

God said to Abraham, "A father of many nations have I made thee" (past tense), and since God put this promise in the past tense, Abraham did the same and acted his faith by taking his new name, "Abraham" which means "the father of a multitude."

A man put a certain amount of money in the pocket of his wife's coat telling her he had done so and asking her if she believed him. She replied, "certainly I do" and began to plan how she would spend it. She actually had this money before she saw it. Why should we believe the bare word of *others* and demand proof from God?

If someone should deed you a home that you had never seen, you actually have a home before you see it. "Faith is the evidence (title deed) of things not (yet) seen." A deed makes a home so much yours that you can sell it without ever seeing it. Faith is believing you *have* what God says you have and acting accordingly before you either feel or see that you have it.

God said to Joshua, "See, I *have* delivered into thy hand Jericho." Joshua and his men put this victory in the past tense as God had done, and the walls of Jericho fell down flat while they were acting their faith.

Jesus said to the ten lepers who asked for mercy, "Go show thyselves unto the priests." His words unto them were as much as to say, "I have given you my word that it is done." They knew the law of the leper and therefore what His command meant. And so they put their healing in the past tense before seeing it, and it was manifested while they were acting their faith.

Jonah put his deliverance in the past tense, called his symptoms "lying vanities" and sacrificed with the voice of thanksgiving while he was still in the stomach of the great fish. It worked.

The reason thousands are not getting what they pray for is that they are keeping their blessing in the future tense which is only HOPE and not *faith* which *takes* the blessings NOW.

"Were the gifts of God for soul and body merely PROMISED gifts, we would have to wait for the Promiser to fulfill His promises, and the responsibility would be on Him. But all of God's blessings are OFFERED gifts as well as promised, and therefore need to be *accepted;* and the responsibility for their transfer is *ours.* This clears GOD of all responsibility for any failures.

The only reason you were not saved a year earlier than you were is that you did not take what God had provided and was offering to you. God was not making you wait; you were making Him wait.

Some say, "God will heal me in His own good time." This is only HOPE and not faith. Faith TAKES what God offers NOW.

9

The Faith That Takes

*"What things soever ye desire, when ye pray, believe
that ye have received them, and ye shall have them."*
MARK 11:24.

Faith a Title-Deed

"Faith is the evidence [or title-deed] to things not seen"
(Heb. 11:1). In Jeremiah, a title-deed is repeatedly spoken
of as "the evidence." Your deed is "the evidence" or proof
that you own your home. So faith is the title-deed to what
you have not *yet* seen. When you have been given a deed
to a home which you have not yet seen, you already have a
home before you see it. Jesus repeatedly said, "He that
believeth, hath." Moffat's translation of Heb. 11:1 reads:
"Faith means we are convinced that we *have* what we do
not see."

In Mark 11:24, Jesus commands us to believe we "have
received" the things we pray for, at the time we pray, without waiting to see or feel them; and on this condition He
promises, "Ye *shall* have them." Faith for the healing of your
body, the same as faith for forgiveness, is to believe, on the
authority of God's Word, that you were forgiven before you
felt forgiven. Nothing else is faith, for "Faith is the evidence
of things *not seen*." As soon as the blessing we take by faith
is *manifested,* faith for *that* blessing ends.

If you are the beneficiary in a rich man's will, you are
already wealthy the moment the rich man dies, though you

have not yet seen any of the money. Just so, everything bequeathed to us in our Lord's Last Will and Testament is already ours by virtue of the death of Jesus, the Testator. Faith is simply using what belongs to us.

In connection with healing, the same as with forgiveness, to believe we "have received" healing at the time we pray, before seeing or feeling it, is the "confidence" which the Holy Spirit, in Heb. 10:35, 36, tells us not to cast away, for the reason that it "hath great recompence of reward." Peter tells us that it is the testing of this faith (the faith that we "have received") which is "more precious than gold."

Believing that our prayer is granted at the time we pray, and that therefore we already have what we prayed for, before we see it, is the "confidence" referred to in I John 5:15, 16: "We *know* that we *have* the petition that we desire of Him."

The fig tree which Jesus cursed, dried up, not from the leaves which could be seen, but "from the roots" which were out of sight. The death of the tree could not be detected, at the first, by looking at the leaves.

Our "Emancipation Proclamation"

Calvary was our "Emancipation Proclamation" from everything outside of the will of God. We are simply to believe what God says He has done for us, and act upon it, taking our blood-bought liberty just as the slaves of the South did after the Emancipation Proclamation by Abraham Lincoln. Suppose the slaves had judged by the evidence of the senses, saying, "I don't feel different; I can't see any change; all my surroundings are just the same as they were." Would that be faith? It was *faith* only when they acted on the freedom which was already theirs.

Just so, by believing and acting on the Word of God, everything that belongs to us in Christ, becomes available at once. To accept any contrary physical evidence in preference to the Word of God, is to nullify the Word, as far as you are concerned. Faith is believing what God says in the face of the contrary evidence of the senses. We are to be "steadfast" in resisting, as reasons for doubting, everything contrary to the Word of God. Faith means that we have left the sense realm.

If a friend should deposit in the bank a hundred thousand dollars to your credit and bring you the pass-book and a check book, you wouldn't examine your empty pocketbook to see how much money you have; you would examine your pass-book. The Bible is the Christian's pass-book. God has deposited in Christ all I need. It is already mine. To neglect it is not a proper attitude toward God. A right attitude toward God and His promises will bring about their fulfillment.

You have to receive Christ before experiencing any of the wonderful results of receiving Him. Christ *first*, *afterwards* the results. We receive healing, divine life and strength, and every other promised blessing in exactly the same way we received Christ and forgiveness. Since forgiveness is invisible, how do you receive it? Answer: by faith in God's Word. Why not receive divine healing, and life and strength in the same way?

Any blessing which is received *by faith*, you must have before you see it—before it is manifested. Otherwise it would not be received by *faith*, which is "the evidence of things not seen." The "ten lepers" already had healing in its unmanifested form when they started on their way to show the priest they were healed." Their healing was manifested while they were acting their faith. God's announcement, "I am the Lord that healeth thee," is to be received as the voice of God, and believed as a present tense fact, and evaluated according to its cost.

The Six Senses

As perfume is non-existent to the sense of hearing, so what we take by faith according to Mark 11:24 is, at first, non-existent to the five natural senses. You do not doubt the existence of what you *see* because you can't *smell* or *taste* or *hear* it; then why doubt the existence of what you have taken by faith (the sixth sense) because you can't *yet see* or *feel it?* The five natural senses belong to "the *natural* man" who, Paul tells us, "cannot know the things of God." It is only by our *sixth* sense—faith—that we can see and take and hold on to the blessings God offers to us until they are fully manifested. To consult our natural senses for evidence that our prayer has been granted is as ridiculous as trying to see with our ears or to hear with our eyes.

All of our six senses work independently of each other; you *see* what you can't hear; you hear what you can't see; etc. Just so you have by faith what is, at first, non-existent to the natural senses. It is important to see that the contrary evidence of the senses is no reason for doubting; because the evidences upon which faith rests are still perfect. It is faith only when we are believing in the face of the contrary evidence of the senses. Abraham received and believed the Word of God in the face of *nature's* evidence to the *impossibility*.

You must already have perfume before you can smell it. You must already have food before you can taste it; and you must already have the healing before you can feel it. Faith receives forgiveness and healing and praises God for them when there is nothing to praise Him for as far as the five senses are *yet* witnesses.

Jesus said, "I thank Thee that Thou hast heard Me," when the raising of Lazarus was yet in an unmanifested form. Just so it is before we see or feel any change that we are to believe that our prayer for healing is granted and we are to say as Jesus did, "I thank Thee that Thou hast heard me." The angels at Dothan were already present before they became visible to the servant of Elisha. The ability God gave him to *see* these angels did not create them.

God works while we maintain the mental habit of faith— "while we look not at the things which are seen, but at the things which are not seen"—at God, at His promises, His faithfulness, His justice, etc. (2 Cor. 4:18). Faith has to do only with the unseen and unfelt. As soon as what we have taken by faith is manifested to the senses, it ceases to be faith.

The Right Mental Attitude

No person who allows his mind to be ruled by his senses can have victorious faith. The mind that is ruled by the senses lives in a realm of uncertainty. Until God's Word gains mastery over your mind, your mind will be swayed by feelings and by things you see or hear, rather than by the Word of God. The mind and thoughts of those seeking healing must be "renewed" so as to be brought into harmony with the mind of God as revealed in the Bible and pointed out in our healing literature. Faith for God's promised blessings is the result of knowing and acting on God's Word. The right mental attitude or the "renewed mind" (Rom. 12:2), makes steadfast faith possible to all. God always heals when He can get the right cooperation.

Having Before Seeing

I put a certain amount of money in Mrs. Bosworth's coat pocket, and later told her I had, asking her if she believed me. She said, "Of course I do," and thanked me for it. She actually had this money before she saw it. Why should we believe the bare word of *others* and demand visible proof from God?

Continue to believe that God gave you what you asked for when you prayed, thanking and praising Him for what He has given, and it will always materialize. This always puts God to working. So many are waiting for God to heal them, when He is waiting for them to take what He is offering them. How trying it would be to a friend who offered you a gift, for you to cry and beg for it, and keep him waiting for you to take it!

Let me put this in another way. Since Jesus commands us to believe we "have received" the things we pray for at the time we pray, and before they take visible form, it is clear that they exist in two forms: first, *invisible,* afterwards, *visible.* First, "believe that ye *have received* them [in their invisible form] and ye *shall* have them [in their visible or material form]."

We have them *first,* in the *faith* realm, *afterwards* in the *sense* realm. So, Jesus, in Mark 11:24, commands us as soon as we pray to believe that we "have received" (in its invisible form) what we pray for, before He changes it into its visible or material form. The angels at Dothan were just as truly present and real in their invisible form as when they became visible to Elisha's servant. The "ten lepers" each had their healing in its invisible form while they were on their way to show the priest their healing in its *visible* and material form.

When Jesus said, "I thank Thee that Thou *hast* heard Me," the raising of Lazarus was complete in the faith realm before it was seen, a few moments later, in the sense or material form. Just so we are to believe that we already have our complete healing in its invisible form before God changes it into its visible or material form. The fact that "faith is the evidence [or title-deed] to things *not seen*," proves that we must already have the things we pray for in their invisible form, before God *can* change them into their *visible or manifested form*.

The entire eleventh chapter of Hebrews records the actions of God's saints in the faith realm *before* the results of their faith took visible form. All the acts of faith are in the realm of the yet unseen. Believing that we have received the things we pray for at the time we pray, is the "confidence" which is to be steadfast and unwavering until God changes the blessings we have taken, from its *invisible* to its visible form.

Walking by faith *is* walking by the kind of sight which sees and is occupied with "eternal" things — with God, with His promises, His faithfulness, and the many other perfect reasons for faith. It was *believing without seeing* that gave Peter "joy unspeakable and full of glory." Nothing he had ever seen gave him as much joy as he now had by believing without seeing.

The sacrifice of praise and the giving of thanks continually is done in the *faith* realm, or before our blessings have been changed into their visible form. Jonah called his symptoms "lying vanities" and sacrificed with the voice of thanksgiving while he was still in the stomach of the great fish. The Israelites sang praises on their way to battle.

10

Our Confession

Many people fail to receive what they pray for because of a lack of understanding about *confession*.

In Hebrews 3:1, Christianity is called a "confession." The Greek word here translated "profession" is the same as the one usually translated "confession."

What It Means

This particular word in the Greek language means "saying the same thing." It means, to believe and say what God says about our sins, our sicknesses, and everything else included in our redemption.

Confession is an *affirmation* of a Bible truth we have embraced. Confession is simply believing with our hearts and repeating with our lips God's own declaration of what we are in Christ.

The Holy Spirit in I Peter 2:24 says: "By His stripes ye were healed." We are to believe and say the same thing When our affirmation is the Word of God, He watches over it to make it good. (Jeremiah 1:12)

Confession is faith's way of expressing itself.

"The High Priest of Our Confession"

In Hebrews 3:1 we are commanded to "consider Christ Jesus the Apostle and High Priest of our confession." As our High Priest Jesus acts in our behalf according to what we confess when it is in accordance with God's Word.

Paul tells us that he preached "the Word of faith," that if thou shalt confess with thy mouth, Jesus *as Lord,* and shalt believe in thy heart that God raised Him from the dead, thou shalt be saved. For with the heart man believeth unto righteousness, and with the mouth confession is made unto salvation" (Romans 10:8).

The Relation of Confession to Manifestation

Notice here that the confession — saying the same thing that God says — is by *faith*; that is, believing and confessing *before* experiencing the result.

The confession comes *first*, and *then* Jesus our High Priest responds with the New Birth. It is not salvation unto confession, but confession unto salvation — confession before salvation.

There is no such thing as salvation without confession.

Faith is acting upon God's Word; and this always puts God to work fulfilling His promise.

What Are We to Confess?

Few Christians today have recognized the place confession holds in God's plan for our appropriation of His blessings. Whenever the word "confession" is used, many instinctively think of confessing sin, weakness, and failure. This is only the negative side of this great question. Our *negative* confession of *sin* was only to open the way for the *positive* confession "unto salvation" — of a whole lifetime of believing with our heart and saying with our lips everything God says to us in His promises.

Confessing unto salvation in its *initial* form, and then in each of its *successive* forms. First in the form of the new birth, then in the form of every blessing promised us in the Word of God. The Christian is to act on every phase of his salvation that he knows about. We are to believe with the heart and confess with our mouth to the extent of the "word of faith" which Paul preached. He preached "all the counsel of God." He preached "the unsearchable riches of Christ." He said that he "kept back nothing that was profitable" unto them.

All that Jesus did in His substitutionary work is the private property of the individual for whom Jesus did it. So throughout our Christian life, God wants us to believe with our heart and say with our lips all He says we are in Christ. We are not to ignore or neglect our *legal* standing in Christ, for it is the basis for the acts of faith which puts God to work fulfilling His Word to us. We are to confess or whisper in our own heart, "In Him I am complete." When we know that God in His Word says, "I am the Lord that healeth thee" we are to believe it and confess it with our lips, and Christ will act as our High Priest and make it good.

We are to confess that Calvary was our "Emancipation Proclamation" from everything outside the will of God, and act accordingly. We are to confess that our sicknesses were laid on Christ, and that we are redeemed from the curse of disease. "Let him that is weak say, I am strong," for "the Lord is my strength."

Our confession includes:

> The whole of Scripture truth;
> All that His sacrifice provided;
> All that His High Priesthood covers;
> The whole of God's revealed will;

We are to confess that our redemption is complete. Satan's dominion is ended; for Calvary has freed us. Like the slaves of the south we are to believe that we are free on the basis of our Emancipation Proclamation, never on the basis of our feelings, or on the evidences of our senses.

Remission is the wiping out of everything connected with the old life. We are a "new creation." The old things have passed away, and all things are become new.

We are to make continual confession of our redemption from Satan's dominion.

Of course we are not to say to others that our healing is fully manifested before it is. God does not say that. But you can say to those who ask you, "I am standing on the Word of God."

Wrong Confession

We never rise above our confession. A negative confession will lower us to the level of that confession. It is what we confess with our lips that really controls us. Our confession imprisons us if it is negative, or sets us free if it is positive. Many are always telling of their failings and their lack of faith. Invariably they go to the level of their confession. Confessing lack of faith increases doubt. Every time you confess doubts and fears, you confess your faith in Satan and deny the ability and grace of God. When you confess doubt, you are imprisoned with your own words. Proverbs 6:2, "Thou art snared with the words of thy mouth, thou art taken captive with the words of thy lips." When we doubt His Word it is because we believe something else that is contrary to that Word. Wrong confession shuts the Father out and lets Satan in.

We are to refuse to have anything to do with wrong confessions. When we realize that we will never rise above our confession, we are getting to the place where God can use us.

Disease gains the ascendancy when you confess the testimony of your senses. Feelings and appearances have no place in the realm of faith. Confessing disease is like signing for a package that the Express Company has delivered. Satan then has the receipt from you showing you have accepted it. Don't accept anything that Satan brings — "Give no place to the devil."

I Peter 4:11, "If any man speak, let him speak as the oracles of God." In Ephesians 4:29, we are commanded to speak only "that which is good to the use of edifying." We are not to testify for the adversary. We are to *act* faith, *speak* faith, and to *think* faith.

In Phil. 4:8 the Holy Spirit says, "Finally, brethren, whatsoever things are true, (the Word is) whatsoever things are just, whatsoever things are pure, whatsoever things are lovely, whatsoever things are of good report; if there be any virtue, and if there be any praise, *think* on these things."

The Holy Spirit says in Proverbs, "as a man thinketh in his heart so is he." In II Corinthians 5:5, the Holy Spirit says, "the weapons of our warfare are mighty—bringing into captivity every thought to the obedience of Christ." We are to "cast down reasonings" and give the Word of God its place in our minds and in our lips.

We are to have "the mind of Christ."

Jesus remembers when He bore your sicknesses, and the Holy Spirit commands, "forget not all His benefits, who forgiveth all thine iniquities, who healeth all thy diseases."

God's spiritual and physical transformations are to come to us "by the renewing of our minds." Romans 12:1, "—present your *bodies* (the home or laboratory of the five senses) a living sacrifice—and be transformed by the renewing of your mind, that ye may prove what is that good, and acceptable, and perfect will of God."

A spiritual law that few recognize is that our confession rules us. It is what we confess with our lips that really dominates our inner being. Make your lips do their duty. Refuse to allow them to destroy the effectiveness of God's Word in your case. Some confess with their lips but deny in their heart. They say "yes, the Word is true," but in their heart they say, "it is not true in my case." The confession of your lips has no value as long as your heart repudiates it.

"Hold Fast Your Confession"

Hebrews 4:14 R.V. "Having then a great High Priest, Who has passed through the heavens, Jesus the Son of God, let us *hold fast* our confession," the confession of our faith in the redemptive work that God wrought in Christ.

I am told to *hold fast* to the confession of the absolute integrity of the Bible. I am told to *hold fast* to the confession of the work of Christ in all its phases. I am told to *hold fast* to the confession that "God is the strength of my life." I am told to *hold fast* to the confession that, "surely He hath borne my sicknesses and carried my diseases" and that "by His stripes I am healed."

God says this, and we are to believe and *say* the same things. We are to know what our rights are as revealed by the Word, and then *hold fast* to our confession of them.

When you know that Christ "took our infirmities and bore our sicknesses" *hold fast* to your confession of it.

When you read "greater is He that is in you than he that is in the world" *hold fast* to this confession.

We are to *hold fast* our confession of what Christ has done *for us,* in order that it may be done *in* us.

We are to *hold fast* to the confession of our redemption from Satan's dominion.

We are to *hold fast to* our confession in the face of all contrary evidence.

God declares that "by His stripes I am healed." I am to confess what God says about my sickness, and *hold fast* to this confession. I am to recognize the absolute truthfulness of these words in advance of any visible change. I am to act on these words and thank Him for the fact that He laid my sickness on Christ the same as He did my sins.

Healing is always in response to faith's testimony. Some fail when things get difficult *because they lose their confession*. Disease, like sin, is defeated by our confession of the Word. Make your lips do their duty; fill them with the Word. Make them say what God says about your sickness. Don't allow them to say anything to the contrary.

Believing God's Word with our heart implies our having "put off the old man" with his habit of judging by the evidence of the senses. Faith regards all contrary symptoms as "lying vanities" as Jonah did, and puts the Word in the place of the senses.

Our only problem is to keep in harmony with God's Word and not allow the senses to usurp the place of the Word. We cease to live with doubting Thomas who says "Except I shall see—I shall not believe." We are to prove Christ's own words, "Blessed are they that have not seen, and yet believe." The Word is lifeless until faith is breathed into it on your lips. *Then* it becomes a supernatural force. Make your lips harmonize with the Word of God.

His High Priestly Office

His High Priestly ministry meets our every need from the moment of our new birth until we enter heaven. Why are we to hold fast our confession?

Because Christ is the High Priest of our Confession, (Heb. 4:4),

Because He is a *"great* High Priest,"

Because He is a *merciful* High Priest,"

Because He is touched with the *feeling* of our infirmities,"

Because He ever liveth "to make intercession for us." He is always ready to give us "grace to help in time of need" (Heb. 4:16).

Our Success Is Assured

Because Jesus is "the High Priest of our Confession." When you confess that "by His stripes I am healed" and hold on to your confession, no disease can stand before you. Just thank the Father and praise Him whenever a need confronts you that is covered by redemption, and it is yours. Faith is thanking God from the heart for healing that has not yet been manifested but that we are as sure of as if it were manifested.

The confession of your lips that has grown out of faith in your heart will absolutely defeat the adversary in every combat. Christ's words broke the power of demons and healed the sick. They do the same thing today when we believe and confess them. The Word will heal you if you continually confess it. God will make your body obey your confession of His Word; for "no word of God is void of power" (Luke 1:37).

If I dare say that Psalm 34:10 is true, "But they that seek the Lord shall not want any good thing" and stand by my confession, God will make good all I have confessed.

Nothing will establish you and build your faith as quickly as confession.

Confess it in your heart first.

Confess it out loud in your room.

Say it over and over again.

Say it until your spirit and your words agree.

Say it until your whole being swings into harmony and into line with the Word of God.

Christ's Words are filled with Himself, and as we act on them, they fill us with Christ. We are to obey the Word as we would obey Jesus if He stood visibly in our presence.

Confessing Christ as Lord

When coming to God for salvation in its initial form, and then in every other form afterwards, our confession of, and surrender to Christ's *Lordship* is required. The Holy Spirit says in Col. 2:6, "As ye have therefore received Jesus *as Lord,* so walk in Him." Rom. 14:9, "For to this end Christ both died and rose, and revived, that He might be *Lord* both of the dead and of the living." Appropriating faith for the fulfillment of any promise implies our surrender to His *Lordship.* It is while we are surrendered to Him *as Lord* over our lives that He is ready:

To heal us,

To baptize us with the Spirit,

To give us "zoe" — God's own life in abundance,

To be within us a fountain springing up unto everlasting life,

To make our legal standing our experience,

To manifest His Person in the form of every blessing promised,

To be Himself our strength, our portion, our all,

To give us the unlimited use of His Name,

To enable us to cast out demons in His Name,

To anoint us for preaching,

To enable us to lay our hands on the sick for their recovery, etc.

Your success and usefulness in the world is going to be measured by your confession and by the tenacity with which you "hold fast" that confession under all circumstances.

God can be no bigger in you than you confess Him to be.

In the face of every need, confess that the Lord is your Shepherd and that you do not want.

* * *

(Most of the thoughts expressed in this sermon I have brought together, by permission, from the writings of Rev. E. W. Kenyon, Author of "The Father and His Family," "The Wonderful Name of Jesus," "Two Kinds of Life," "Jesus The Healer," "In His Presence," "Two Kinds of Love," "Two Kinds of Faith," "Two Kinds of Righteousness," and "Kenyon's Living Poems." Mr. Kenyon's P. O. Address is, Box 145, Seattle, Wash.)

11

Fullness of God's Life the Secret of Victory

Without a divine revelation I cannot tell a person the specific reason why their prayer for the fulfillment of a divine promise is delayed. I can, however, point you to a most wonderful truth — the most vital of all truths, that God has revealed — and which is the only cure for all our ailments.

A delay in receiving healing for instance is, in one sense, good news — the good news that we can have more of "The Life of God."

There are four Greek words in the New Testament, translated "Life." One of these means, "Manner of Life"; another means "Human Life"; another "Behaviour"; but the Greek word for the kind of Life that Jesus brought to the world is "zoe,'" translated, "Eternal Life," and "The Life of God." "Eternal Life" is the actual Life of the Eternal Himself.

The gospel of John opens with the word "zoe." This word is found in the New Testament one-hundred and thirty times. St. John 10:10 tells us that man was to have a right to an abundance of a new kind of life — "God's Own Life," new, of course, only in the sense of human possession.

The Life That Lives Itself

Many ministers today major "Manner of Life" and "Behavior" rather than "zoe," — "The Life of God" which, when received in sufficient measure, lives itself. Paul prayed for Christians, already filled with the Spirit, that they "might be filled with all the fullness of God." This shows that "zoe" is God Himself, and all we have of it is an unsevered part of "The Life of God."

The way to be "full of faith" is to be full of that kind of Life which "believeth all things."

The way to be full of divine love is to be full of "The Life of God," Who is love.

"All things are possible" to "zoe." When it is received in sufficient measure, it can fulfill in us any promise or any requirement in the Bible. To fulfill in us all that the Bible requires or promises, is precisely what "The Life of God" in us was to accomplish. By receiving enough of the "Life of God," we can be made "more than conquerors," "spirit, soul, and body." God wants to do *in* us all that He did in Christ *for* us.

"Zoe" received in sufficient measure transforms us "from glory to glory into the image of Christ." It turns belief into knowledge. It is the source of all the divine graces. It gives us God's wisdom. It overcomes "the world, the flesh, and the devil." It works in us "that which is well-pleasing in His sight."

It is by filling us with His own Life that God Himself becomes our Life, our peace, our righteousness, our purity, our strength, our health, and the Preserver of "our whole spirit, soul, and body," our zeal, our joy, our faith, our Guide, our Teacher, our satisfaction, and our "everything that pertains to life and Godliness."

God's Blessings Are a Part of Himself

By filling us with more and more of His Life, God wants to manifest Himself in us in the form of every spiritual blessing He has promised. This is the miracle and the genius of Christianity. Rom. 5:10 tells us, that we are "saved by His Life." This is true for both soul and body.

It is impossible to measure up to God's purpose for our prayer life without being full of that Life that "ever liveth to make intercession." In other words, it is when "zoe" inspires our prayers that we can ask what we will and receive it. "Zoe" — the "Life of God" is the Healer of soul and body. Divine healing, divine life, and divine strength is Christ *Himself* "made manifest in our mortal flesh." The fullness of this new Life is better than the healing it produces. David said, "the *Lord* is my portion," "the Lord is my strength," etc. etc. His blessings were God manifesting *Himself* in these various forms. God gives us each spiritual blessings by giving us Himself — our blessings are a part of God.

Jesus said, "I am the Vine and ye are the branches." The Vine's life is "The Life of the branches is a part of the life of the Vine. It is Christ's will that all the branches shall be *full* of His own Life. When we are *full* of "zoe" we are one with God just as the bay is one with the ocean because the tides flow into the bay. Paul says, "they that are joined to the Lord are one spirit". That is to say, our spirit and His Spirit are blended into one. This truth provides us with one of the answers to the question "why am I not healed?"

I have heard Christians express their reasons for wanting to be filled with the Spirit. It seems to me that every Christian in the world would pray until they were filled with the Spirit if they knew the many glorious reasons why the Holy Spirit wants them to be filled with Himself. One of His reasons is that He wants to be unhindered in His wonderful work of quickening continually our whole spirit, soul and body. In John 6:63, Jesus said, "It is the Spirit that quickeneth," or giveth Life. He is spoken of in Romans as "The Spirit of Life". All life is due to the direct action of the Holy Spirit. It is His work to impart to us continually the actual Life of Jesus, who is the true source of Life for both the souls and bodies of God's children. When we are anything less than FULL of the Spirit, which is the condition of His perfect working, His work of quickening of increasing the Divine life in our spirit, soul, and body, is hindered or limited.

Jesus said that He came, not only that we might have Life, but that we might have it "more abundantly". And we cannot have His Life in the measure which He desires unless we are filled with the Spirit. The abiding which Christ commanded keeps us filled with the Spirit, thus removing from us all hindrances to the Spirit's constant quickening. In the 11th Psalm, Davis used the word "quicken" eleven times. He knew that more Life is the cure — the only cure—for all our ailments. It is well to know what we pray for. David desired quickening—more Life—increased Life. He therefore sought that blessing which is the root of all the rest. He prayed, "Quicken me after Thy loving-kindness." We need never fear anything that loving-kindness does. Nothing else is so good; and loving-kindness itself cannot do us a greater service than by making us to have "Life more abundantly."

"According to Thy Word"

In the 25th verse of this Psalm — the 119th — David prayed, "Quicken Thou me according to Thy Word." Thank God, we can all pray with faith and get the answer, every day, to this comprehensive and inspired prayer, "Quicken Thou me according to Thy Word." Notice that the quickening is, as David said, "ACCORDING TO THY WORD." The Holy Spirit inspired the Word of God, and it is His own blueprint to which He works, while carrying on His great work of quickening. So to be quickened "according to God's Word," means to be full of His Life in the entire range of our complex being, body, soul and spirit.

God has made Christ the treasury of all that He is. In Him is "all the fulness of the Godhead bodily," and we can be full of everything that the Vine contains. The abiding branch not only has life, but is FULL of life all the time. It is by the Spirit's fulness and the consequent unhindered quickening that we are "preserved", as Paul says, "spirit, soul and body." Paul says, the Spirit will "quicken ALSO your mortal body,"' and in 2 Corinthians 4:11 we have the words, "that the Life also of Jesus might be made manifest in our mortal flesh." If you need healing from Christ, wait on God for the Spirit to quicken you to the extent that Mark 11:24 shall be fulfilled in you. This is exactly what the Divine Quickener wants to do for you.

Let us pray, every day. "Quicken Thou me (give me more Life) ACCORDING TO THY WORD," that is, according to every revelation we find in the Bible which shows us ourselves as God wants us to be. Every time you discover in the Word more than what God requires, rejoice and be encouraged, because it is the work of the Spirit—not your work—to quicken you just to that extent. Let this prayer be your first prayer every day, for it is the condition of a thousand other blessings. It is God's way of "fulfilling in you all the good pleasure of His goodness". The Holy Spirit wants to quicken us to the extent that everything He has revealed concerning us in God's Word shall be fulfilled in us.

In the 50th verse of this 119th Psalm David says, "Thy Word hath quickened me." The Spirit quickens us according to our trust in God's Word — according, or to the extent, of every promise or command that we find from time to time in the Word of God. This quickening will be, as Paul says, "from glory to glory." God's words "are spirit and life" to accomplish exactly what they reveal. When we pray to be quickened "according to His *Word*" we know that we are praying according to His *will* and can therefore obtain the answer. "According to His Word" means according to both His promises and His commands. The more the Word requires, the better, for the greater will be the quickening. What a glorious privilege it is that whenever we feel the least lack, we can pray to the Giver of Life, "Quicken Thou me"— Give me more Life. We need quickening every day. While on earth Jesus said, "Come to me and drink"; and from Heaven He is still saying in the last chapter of the Bible, "Whosoever will, let him take of the water of Life freely." He wants to be an inexhaustable fountain of Life within us springing up and flowing out in "rivers of living water."

(The repeated reading and whole-hearted daily practice of this message will make possible the fulfilment, in you, of any promise or requirement in the Bible. Its practice is an increasing blessing to me every day, and always will be.— F. F. B.)

12

God's Garden

"I did the planting, Apollos did the watering, but it was God who made the seed grow . . . you are God's field to be planted" (I Cor. 3:6-9 — Moffatt's translation).

How to Get God's Promises Fulfilled

Every moral being on earth has been "bought with a price" to be the Lord's garden in which His "imperishable seed" is to grow and be cultivated and produce its wonders. Real Christians are God's "farm" — His "husbandry"—-His "field" — His "garden." A "field" belongs to its owner. So Paul says, "Ye are not your own; ye are bought with a price." God holds the title deed. We are absolutely His. We belong to Him by right of creation and by right of preservation. But the greatest fact is that we belong to Him by right of redemption — because He "bought" us with an infinite price, to be His "field."

The Planting of the Seed

Paul said to the Corinthians, "I did the planting." In the parable of the sower, Jesus said, "The seed is the Word." It is the "imperishable seed." God brings about His wonderful harvests in the same way a farmer does. Jesus said, "He sent forth a sower to sow." It is God's Word that lets us know what to trust Him for. "Faith cometh by hearing" — by our knowing what God's will is for us. Because they can accomplish such wonders, God wants all His "seed" planted. God's purpose in creating seed was that it might be planted in

155

"good ground" where it could germinate and "grow" and "bring forth fruit." So Paul said, "I did the planting." Seed is powerless until it is planted.

The infinite price God paid for the "field" reveals the importance of planting the "imperishable seed." All of God's wonderful works are potentially in the "seed." David said, "All His work is done in faithfulness," that is, in faithfulness to His promises. God's works are prevented until the seed is in "good ground." His design for us all is that we spend our lives making possible the germination and growth of the "imperishable seed." Nothing can take the place of the seed, not even prayer. Prayer is not the seed; the Word is the seed. The only purpose of God's promises is their fulfillment. They are all a revelation of what He is eager to do for us. The Holy Spirit, whose work it is to fulfill the promises, speaks of them as "exceeding great and precious." Their greatness is seen in their suitableness to meet all our needs and to fill all our capacities. Their immutability makes them "exceeding great and precious," because it removes all reason for doubt and gives us perfect reasons upon which to base our expectations. As "seed," they cannot be changed. They therefore accomplish their wonderful results at any time and in any garden.

It is the business of Christians to prove to the world by actual demonstration that the promises of God are as true today as they were two thousand years ago. They were given to be known and recognized, claimed, and pleaded in prayer. They are to be sown and tilled by prayer. In Romans 4:12, God speaks of Christians as those "who also walk in the steps of that faith of our father Abraham," meaning that we should all treat every promise God has made to us exactly as Abraham treated God's promise to him. Can it be that God is less real to men of this Holy Spirit dispensation than He was to those who lived in the shadows of these "better things"?

Jesus said to some of the Jews in His day, "My word hath no place in you." What place should the Word of God have in us? I answer that it ought to obtain and retain an inside place in the thoughts, the memory, the conscience, and the affections. It ought to obtain and retain in us a place of honor, reverence, faith, love, and obedience. It ought to obtain and retain in us a place of trust. It ought to obtain and retain in us a place of authority.

Millions of people sing that glorious hymn "Standing on the Promises of God," while the fact is that most of God's promises are never claimed by most modern church-members. Standing on the promises of God means to get them fulfilled; it means to appropriate the blessing that each promise reveals; it means to pray "the prayer of faith" for their fulfillment. Neglecting them is equivalent to undoing what their fulfillment would mean if it were already accomplished. Their preciousness should determine our love and esteem of them. Paul was glad to say, "I did the planting." If all farmers treated their seed as millions of church-members today treat God's "imperishable seed," the world would starve to death.

The Possibilities in the Seed

In the seed there are infinite possibilities. This is why it should be said of every one, as it was at the beginning, "They gladly received the Word." In the plainest Bible text there is a world of blessing, just as in a little seed there is a potential tree a million times bigger than the seed. One verse of Scripture allowed to germinate in a human heart may grow into a harvest of thousands of conversions and the "eternal glory" which follows. One kernel of wheat can, in time, cover a continent and feed nations; and the results of cultivating the "imperishable seed" are as much greater and more desirable than the harvests of material seed as the heavens are higher than the earth. Only the "imperishable seed" can bring about imperishable results. The Bible says: "Every seed bringeth forth after its kind." Each promise, by the blessing promised, reveals the nature of the harvest of promises fulfilled.

The Watering

Paul said, "I did the planting; BARNABAS DID THE WATERING." All the seed and all the plants in God's garden need watering. Jesus said of the stony ground upon which the seed fell, "It had no moisture." He said, "The seed had no root." If the seed is to grow, the ground must be kept moist. It is because of the lack of constant watering that many of God's plants are withered instead of growing. A garden is a place for growth. Paul wrote to the Corinthians, "Your faith *groweth* exceedingly." "Your love *groweth*." He commanded all to *"grow* in grace." "Therefore, God says to every one of His little gardens, "Be filled with the Spirit"— Keep the ground moist. The water is the Spirit "whom God hath given to them that obey Him." The fullness of the Spirit is the condition of His perfect working.

How David Watered the Seed

Every one of the 176 verses of the 119th Psalm shows David's attitude toward the Word of God. He joyfully acknowledges his obligations to keep God's precepts diligently. He promised: "I will keep Thy statutes." He said to God, "Thy word have I hid in mine heart . . . I have rejoiced in the way of Thy testimonies as much as in all riches . . . I will meditate in Thy precepts . . . Princes also did sit and speak against me; but Thy servant did meditate in Thy statutes . . . I will delight myself in Thy statutes . . . I will not forget Thy Word . . . I have kept Thy testimonies

. . . I have chosen the way of truth . . . I will run the way
of Thy commandments . . . I will observe Thy laws with
my whole heart . . . I delight in Thy commandments . . .
I will keep Thy law continually for ever and ever . . . I
will speak of Thy precepts . . . The proud have had me
greatly in derision: yet have I not declined from Thy law
. . . Thy statutes have been my song . . . Thou art my
portion, O Lord . . . I made haste and delayed not to keep
Thy commandments . . . The proud have forged a lie
against me: but I have kept Thy precepts with my whole
heart . . . The law of Thy mouth is better unto me than
thousands of gold and silver . . . Thy law is my delight . . .
For ever, O Lord, Thy Word is settled in Heaven . . . Thy
faithfulness is unto all generations . . . Unless Thy law had
been my delights, I should then have perished in mine affliction . . . I will never forget Thy precepts . . . O Lord, how
love I Thy law! it is my meditation all the day . . . I have
refrained my feet from every evil way, that I might keep Thy
Word . . . How sweet are Thy Words unto my taste! yea,
sweeter than honey to my mouth! . . . Thy word is a lamp
unto my feet, and a light unto my path . . . I have sworn,
and I will perform it, that I will keep Thy righteous judg-
ments . . . Thy testimonies have I taken as an heritage for
ever: for they are the rejoicing of my heart . . . I have in-
clined my heart to perform Thy statutes always, even unto
the end . . . I hate vain thoughts; but Thy law do I love
. . . I will have respect unto Thy statutes continually . . .
I love Thy commandments above gold; yea, above fine gold
. . . I esteem all Thy precepts concerning all things to be
right; and I hate every false way . . . Thy testimonies are
wonderful: therefore doth my soul keep them . . . Many
are my persecutors and mine enemies; yet do I not decline
from Thy testimonies . . . my heart standeth in awe of Thy

Word . . . I rejoice at Thy Word, as one that findeth great spoil." All of these statements, and many more, are in this 119th Psalm. They show us how David watered the Word. Paul said, "The planter and the waterer are equal." *Watering* the seed is as necessary as *planting* it. God can't make the seed grow unless we water it.

God Makes the Seed Grow

And then Paul said, "It is God who made the seed grow." He made His promises for this one purpose. He *always* makes the seed grow when it is kept in good ground and *watered*. The *growing* comes after the *watering*.

Jesus also said, "It bringeth forth fruit." It *always* brings forth fruit. The intensity of all holy desire is measured by the degree of divine love which one possesses. *God's* desire, therefore, is as much greater than ours can be as His love is greater than ours. His benevolence is so great that His eyes "run to and fro throughout the whole earth" continually seeking opportunities to bless those whose attitude of heart makes it possible. What God has promised *belongs* to us. The justice of God requires that He make the seed grow when it is "planted" and "watered." John says, "He is faithful and just." The word "just" means God would be unjust to withhold from us what He promises. We have a *right* to what He promises us. It is a one hundred per cent fact that God makes every seed grow when it is "planted" and "watered." We can all prove this to our present and eternal delight. God is the best farmer in the universe. He never fails!

God's Time Is Now

Since the work of the "imperishable seed" is *supernatural* and it is "God alone who makes the seed grow," they often produce their wonderful results the same day they are "planted." God's promises are for TODAY; His TIME is always TODAY.

"TODAY if ye will hear His voice, harden not your hearts"
(Heb. 4:7). If you delay the acceptance of God's promises,
you may not be alive tomorrow. The promises of God belong
to us TODAY, and we are not sure of them any other time.
The only way to be sure of God's promised blessings is to
accept HIS TIME; and we read in 2 Cor. 6:2, "Behold NOW
is the accepted time." Since NOW is the time God accepts,
we should accept it as *our* time. He commands us to hear
His voice "TODAY," and says "Harden not your hearts" by
waiting. In Mark 11:24, Jesus said "Believe that ye receive"
(literally "TAKE"). WHEN? "NOW"—"when ye pray."
Faith says, before the answer is manifested, "Father, I thank
Thee that Thou hast heard me." When you cannot SEE or
FEEL, say, "This is the time to trust." The results are not
to be manifested until after we believe our prayer is heard
and continue to believe. Say to God: "Thou art now working
in response to my faith—I count on Thy faithfulness." The
matter passes out of our hands into God's hands the moment
we make a definite committal of it to God. Paul said, "He
is able to keep that which *I have committed* unto Him."
But God does not promise to keep anything that is not committed to Him. This is the way to receive everything God
has promised to us. Were the gifts of God for soul and body
merely PROMISED gifts, we would have to wait for the
Promiser to fulfill His promises, and the responsibility would
be on Him. But all of God's blessings are OFFERED gifts
as well as promised, and therefore need to be ACCEPTED;
and the responsibility for their transfer is OURS. This clears
God of all responsibility for any failure.

The Effect of Watering the Seed

What was the effect of David's attitude toward God's Word
—of his watering the seed? This shepherd boy, by watering
the Word within him, became "wiser than all his teachers."

His attitude toward God's Word made him "a man after God's own heart." It made him the world's greatest Psalmist. His Psalms have blessed millions during the centuries which have followed. His watering of the seed made him a divinely inspired writer. As every seed planted, in turn, produces *more seed,* so David's words in the Psalms became God's "imperishable seed" which have for centuries germinated in human hearts all over the world. His words have been the texts for thousands of sermons.

David found that meditation chews our spiritual food, and gets the sweetness and nutritive virtue of the Word into our hearts and lives. Meditation has a digesting power, and turns truth into spiritual nourishment. It is the Word of God which Paul says "effectually worketh in us" all the divine transformations from "glory to glory." David said, "I understand more than the ancients because I keep Thy precepts." By observing in heart and life the precepts of the Lord, David early in life understood more than those who lived in earlier times learned in a whole lifetime by experience. David, who started life only as a shepherd boy, by meditating in and practicing divine precepts, obtained such wisdom and knowledge that he was spoken of in 2 Samuel 14:17 as "an angel of God" in judging right and wrong. In the same chapter, his wisdom is compared to "the wisdom of an angel." He said, "Thy Word hath quickened me." It quickened his whole being to the extent that God's Word was fulfilled in him. His life was filled wtih praise and thanksgiving. How much better to be the Lord's garden than the devil's. The possibilities of the "imperishable seed" are infinite. Nothing can be so beneficial as being God's garden. Only God can know what the eternal harvest will be. Remember that throughout your Christian life, "YOU ARE GOD'S FIELD TO BE PLANTED."

13

Why Some Fail to Receive Healing
from Christ

Twenty-Two Reasons For Failure To Be Healed

Since it is so clearly revealed everywhere throughout the
Scriptures that the Heavenly Father wills our healing, why do
some in our day, who seek healing, fail to receive it? This
is a question in the minds of many honest inquirers. There
are several answers to this question, which we will mention
briefly, since by these answers many who had failed to receive
healing have been enabled to locate themselves, after which
they have been gloriously healed:

1. *Insufficient instruction — Ignorance concerning the
healing power of the Gospel.*

Paul tells us that "faith cometh by hearing, and hearing
by the Word of God." Many have sought healing from
Christ before having heard or known enough of the Word
of God to produce in them a steadfast faith. The early Church
members were in one accord in the matter of proclaiming
all the Gospel. They "kept back nothing that was profitable."
They declared "all the counsel of God."

We have seen that God's way of producing *faith for healing*
is the same as that of producing *faith for salvation,* or for
any other blessing, and that is for the needy one first to learn
from the Scriptures what is God's will in the matter. The
hand of faith cannot reach out and take from God what the

163

eye of faith does not first see to be the will of God. Jesus
said, "Ye shall know the truth, and the truth shall make you
free." It is the truth of the Written Word that sets us free
—the truth known, understood, received, acted upon, main-
tained and steadfastly believed with an appropriating faith.

Paul tells us that it is "the Word of God, which effectually
worketh in (them) that believe." The Word of God is the
"precious seed," the "imperishable seed," the "seed" that has
the power and which never fails to do its own work when
known and *received* and *kept* in "the good ground" in which
alone good seed can grow.

Some fail to receive healing because they are trying to get
results from the seed (the Word concerning healing) without
knowing what that Word is and without giving it its place
and keeping it in "the good ground" in which alone it can
do its work. The seed cannot work *in* us unless it *is in us*
by our having known and received it.

Before saying, "I am the Lord that healeth thee," and
promising to take away all our sicknesses, God *first* said, "If
thou wilt diligently hearken . . . and do all." This means,
to be diligent in the matter of knowing, understanding and
practicing what God has to say in His Word on the subject
of healing. *We must know what God offers to us before we*
can expect it from Him. The knowledge of God's will must
precede faith for that will to be done. Multitudes today do
not know that the perfect healing of their bodies is the fully
revealed will of God in His Written Word, the Bible. To
know this, is the *only sufficient evidence for appropriating*
faith.

Unless those seeking healing can say, when tested, "It is
written," and then can quote to the adversary a promise
which settles the question of God's will, their faith cannot
remain steadfast. Multitudes of sufferers who have prayed

for healing for years without success, because of having used in their prayers *the faith-destroying phrase,* "IF it be Thy will," have afterwards been healed through the truth of God's Word contained and explained in this book.

The early Church members were not only in one accord in teaching this subject but also they lifted up their voices to God in one accord in prayer for "signs and wonders" of healing, praying "the prayer of faith" before the sick were brought into the streets of Jerusalem. It was not the faith of *a single evangelist,* but the faith of *the entire company of believers* that brought healing to *"everyone"* in the streets of Jerusalem after Christ's ascension (Acts 5:14-16).

The majority of ministers and church members of today through their ignorance of and their traditions on the subject of the ministry of healing, are opposed to it as it was taught and preached and practiced in the early Church.

Instead of praying with one accord for these healing results as the early Church members did, the present Church members as a whole have not accepted our Lord's attitude toward sickness as revealed in the Gospels. In our day opposition often takes the place of united prayer; unbelief takes the place of united faith; lukewarmness takes the place of being Spirit-filled, as all the early Church members were. So I will ask *you* the question: May not the blame for the failure of some to receive healing today be largely due to the unbelieving part of the Church itself, since we are members one of another? I believe you will say, Yes, to this.

Suppose it were generally believed that the day of regeneration has passed, as we so often hear it said "the day of miracles has passed." How this would hinder the work of the ministry in that part of the Gospel! Christian workers could have no success in saving souls except by getting people to give up the false tradition and putting the Word of God in its place. On the other hand, suppose that from infancy up we had all been taught the healing part of the Gospel, as definitely as any other part. In this case, I am sure, very few would have any difficulty in evidencing faith for healing.

It is the Word of God which produces faith for healing. We have had the joy of seeing hundreds healed while they were listening to the truth on that subject; others have been healed while reading our printed instructions, which answered their questions and removed the hindrances to their faith.

2. *The second reason why some fail to receive healing is an enlargement on what we have already said.*

Christ planned to carry on His healing ministry during His absence by means of the whole Church, which is His Body, not through an obscure member of that Body. He said, "These signs shall follow THEM"—*the Church*, not "him"—the individual. It was not the faith of a lone or solitary evangelist but that of a Spirit-filled Church as a whole which brought healing to all the sick in the streets of Jerusalem after Christ had gone away, and had sent His successor, the Holy Spirit.

Some do not like public healing services; but here, God, when He had His way, had the multitudes healed right on the streets. He wanted His compassion to be made known too the world as a basis for faith. God began His works in this dispensation as He wants them continued; and that is, through the whole church; with every member *filled* and *kept filled* with the Holy Spirit.

The greatest number of conversions, for instance, are brought about by an outpouring of the Holy Spirit and through a Church in one accord; and this is the way that all were healed in the streets of Jerusalem.

God's wholesale dealings with men, both in saving and healing, is by the outpouring of His Spirit and through a Spirit-filled, united and praying Church. His method is revealed by the promise, "I will pour out My Spirit," and the statement, "They were all filled with the Spirit." A Spirit-filled and praying Church produces an atmosphere in which it is easy for God to work and hard for the devil to interfere; because *this atmosphere is the Holy Spirit Himself,* who is more than a match for the devil.

In the revival belt, during the Finney and other great revivals, sinners were put under conviction as soon as they would step off the train where a revival was in progress. Mr. Finney tells of such a unity in prayer that every adult person on a street three miles long was saved, except one. The Christians unitedly prayed for that one, and he was saved.

It is true that individuals, here and there, are saved and healed where there are no revivals; but God's *regular* way is for His people all to pray for an outpouring of the Holy Spirit. We read, "These all continued in one accord in prayer and supplication." How seldom do we see such a thing now!

Some of our theology today, causes many people to anchor in past blessings without a daily renewing of the fulness which constituted the initial blessing, when they, as Christians, were filled with the Spirit. Unless the Church is filled and kept filled with the Holy Spirit it is impossible that the spiritual atmosphere of the meetings can be what it must be if God is not to be limited or hindered. In this atmosphere, produced by the whole Church being filled with the Spirit and all praying for the work of Christ, the power of God is present to heal as it was at the beginning. God's way is for the whole Church to be filled and kept filled with the same Holy Spirit which saved and healed those multitudes in New Testament times.

Christ the Healer

The results of the fulfillment of Divine promises are the same in any age. If you want to know how the Spirit acts now, just read how He *did* act when He had full possession of the Church. The Book of Acts is a blueprint by which the Holy Spirit wishes to work throughout His dispensation. As the early Christians in Acts 4 were all filled with the Spirit and all prevailed in prayer for "signs and wonders" of healing, so in James 5 all Christians are commanded to pray for the healing of the sick, and to do it as earnestly as Elijah prayed for rain. When this was done in the early Church, "the prayer of faith" by the *elders* was but voicing the prayer of the whole Church.

John says, "This is the confidence that we have in Him, that if we ask anything according to His will, He heareth us." This was proven by the whole company of Christians in the fourth chapter of The Acts. *Every Christian today is commanded to be filled with the Spirit, to pray for the outpouring of the Spirit, and to prevail in prayer for the healing of the sick.* Every priest should be exercising his priesthood, but the failure of the majority to do this in our day, pollutes the atmosphere of the meetings and makes it harder for the sick to have faith and for the Holy Spirit to work.

The failure of the Christians to live and walk in the Spirit, limits the Holy One of Israel; because *our being filled with the Spirit is the condition for His perfect working.* Instead of being surrounded by this atmosphere in our day, a poor, afflicted wife often is surrounded with opposition from her own family and often from her own pastor and fellow church members; and so she fails to receive healing, being too weak in mind and body to fight the battle alone. The very ones who are opposing her are the ones who ought to be praying in faith for her healing. We are *all* to "bear one another's burdens, and so fulfill the law of Christ."

Usually today it is the very ones who are violating these conditions which were met by the early Church who are asking why some fail to receive healing; and the answer is, Because these very doubters are making it impossible for the Church to be in one accord in prayer and faith for the sick. The Church is out of tune with God's program.

In a remarkable document signed by twenty bishops of the Episcopal Church in the Commonwealth of Australia, is given a wonderful report of the miracles of healing manifested in the cathedrals of that Church in various cities in Australia. In this report they say, *"The faith which is needed is not merely individual but corporate faith, the faith of the home, of the ministry and of the whole Church. The Body, not a lone member of it, must cooperate with Christ its Head if its sick members are all to be healed. The most marked groups after the mission, came from parishes where the wave of intercession had been highest and swept farthest . . . The world today is waiting for afresh revelation of the presence and power of God in the work of the Church and in the life of its members. It has already seen and felt once more the wonder of Divine healing."*

Today, a large part of the members of the Church, through ignorance, are opposing that for which the early Church prevailed in prayer. They have not accepted our Lord's attitude towards sickness, and have not met the conditions for the healing of the sick which God desires, and it is these very hinderers who are pointing out the failures for which they themselves are largely responsible.

It is not uncommon today to find those who ought to be doing the works of Christ warning the sick to stay away from places where the works of Christ are being done. Would it not be better for them to warn the people against going where confirmation or baptism or church membership or reformation are put in the place of the new birth?

3. *The third reason why some fail to receive healing from Christ is community unbelief.*

Although in other places Jesus worked miracles and healed all that were sick, when He came to Nazareth, His home town, where He had been brought up, "He could do no miracles there . . . because of their unbelief" (Mark 6:5, 6, Weymouth's Translation). Think of it! Christ Himself, under the full anointing of the Holy Ghost, was *hindered by community unbelief.* Since this is true, is it strange that some in any city, *today,* should fail to receive healing? God would not then allow the gift of miracles to operate through Christ where, by their unbelief, the people were making Him a liar, so why should He do so today? Paul, among the heathen, had better success in working miracles than Jesus had in His home town (Acts 14).

The traditions which the people of today have been taught to believe in the place of the plain Word of God on the subject of healing have turned the whole world into a veritable Nazareth of unbelief. I mean by that, that today community unbelief is almost general. Those who preach the full Gospel and pray for the sick are obliged to labor in a Nazareth of unbelief. We can get results only so far as we can get rid of the "traditions of the elders" regarding healing by teaching the people what the Scriptures actually teach on the subject. By doing this, I boldly say that Jesus Christ (not ourselves) has had greater success in working miracles in all the cities where our revival campaigns have been conducted than He had in Nazareth, His own home town. Now, don't misquote me. I am not saying that *we* have had success. I am talking about what Christ has done, whenever and wherever the people have been enlightened by our ministry so as to know their privilege in the matter of healing.

Did the fact that Christ could do no miracle in Nazareth prove anything but the unbelief of the people? And in passing, if, as some are teaching, the sick are to be healed *without their faith,* why didn't Jesus go ahead and heal the sick in Nazareth? The Bible answers, "because of their unbelief."

If it is proper to account for the failure of some to receive healing by calling in question Christ's willingness to heal all sick persons, then why should we not call in question His willingness to save all sinners in order to explain the fact that so many in the churches are unsaved?

Upon a certain occasion only one woman in a great throng touched Jesus with faith for healing. Later on, whole multitudes did so. It is a matter of enlightenment and faith.

After the nine disciples had failed to deliver the epileptic boy mentioned in the Gospels, some theologian of that day —if he were like many of the theologians of these days— might have seized upon that failure and said, "There, now we have the proof that it is not always God's will to heal." But the father wanted the boy to be healed, the boy, himself, wanted to be healed, and the disciples, Divinely commissioned to cast out devils and heal the sick, wanted him to be healed; yet under similar circumstances today some one would say, because of such a failure, "It is not God's will that such an one should be healed." They would make theology out of the failure. But Jesus came down from the mountain and delivered the boy, thus proving it to be God's will to heal even when His accredited representatives have failed to heal. *Why not make theology out of this?*

When the father of this boy said to Jesus, "If Thou canst do anything," Jesus refused to take the responsibility for any failure. He said, "If thou canst believe," and then the father cried out, "Lord, I believe; help Thou mine unbelief," and, of course, he received the help asked for and succeeded where the apostles, themselves, had failed, for Christ delivered the boy.

Considering the fact that in the healing ministry, we are compelled to labor in the face of almost universal unbelief, and that those who preach only the soul salvation part of the Gospel are laboring in the midst of the almost universal acceptance of that doctrine, I think that God is giving proofs of Divine Healing as bright and convincing as the proofs of regeneration, and that with not nearly so much teaching to produce faith. When I consider the lack of teaching on Divine Healing, and the unspiritual condition of the churches and their general attitude towards this part of forgotten orthodoxy, instead of wondering why some are not healed, I marvel at the success God is giving to those who pray for the sick. I have seen many deaf mutes healed when scarcely a person in the audience expected the healing.

Are not the thousands who now testify that they have been divinely healed in as good health physically as the general average of professing Christians in any church are spiritually? Would not the *physical* health of those who testify that they have been divinely healed compare favorably with the *spiritual* health of those who oppose the Gospel of Healing? Is the average professed Christian any better proof of the doctrine of regeneration than those who testify to having been divinely healed are of the doctrine of Divine Healing? They ought to be, because they have heard that part of the Word of God all their life, whereas the majority of those we pray for, who are healed, have heard the plain teaching of the Word of God concerning Divine Healing for only a few days. There are many today who have been divinely healed after having been deaf and dumb from birth, who can hear better *physically* than the average church member can hear *spiritually*. I have seen many who could not walk a step until after they had been prayed for, who are now walking better *physically* than the average Christian is walking *spiritually;* yet the average Christian all his life has heard the Word of God which teaches the healing of the *soul,* whereas these others have heard only a few times the Word of God which teaches the healing of the *body.*

Are all who have been baptized washed from all their sins? No, but those who have faith are: and what water is in the ordinance of Christian baptism, oil is in the ordinance of anointing the sick for healing.

Suppose some one should say to me, "So-and-so was anointed, but was not healed." I would answer, "So-and-so was baptized, but was not saved—was not healed from the disease of sin." If a man should say to me, "I know a man whom you anointed whose body was not healed," I would say to him, "I know a man whom you baptized whose soul was not healed." Thousands who have been baptized have never been regenerated, and this is infinitely worse than for a Christian to fail to receive healing for his body.

Some say, "If so-and-so should be healed, I will believe in Divine Healing." Why not be consistent, then, and say, "If so-and-so should get saved, I will believe in salvation?" This is the same as to say, "I will believe so-and-so's experience in preference to God and the Bible, and the experiences of all the other thousands who have been saved and healed." After God has healed thousands from all their afflictions, why not say to Him, "I will not believe unless you heal one more."

Would you reject the doctrine of consecration because some church members are not consecrated while thousands of others are? I heard a minister say, concerning the work of another evangelist, "So-and-so was anointed and prayed for, but died without being healed." Yet this same minister baptized so-and-so and took him into the Church, thereby proclaiming to the world that his soul had been healed from the disease of sin, but the man died without the new birth, and his soul was lost. This is infinitely worse than for a sick Christian to fail to be healed and so to die and wake up in glory.

If the testimony of those of us who say we have been healed is to be rejected because, after a careful examination by a medical expert, it could be shown that we fall short of physical perfection, then, to be consistent, why should we not have a spiritual expert with spiritual discernment—such as the apostle Paul had—examine those in the modern Church who oppose the Gospel of Healing and reject the testimony of all those among them who do not measure up spiritually to what the Bible represents a healthy soul to be?

While, after witnessing the miraculous healing of very many thousands, I am convinced that the proofs of healing are as bright and convincing as are the proofs of regeneration, yet I do not base any doctrine on these answers to prayer. I for one will preach all the Gospel if I never see another man saved or healed as long as I live. I am determined to base my doctrines upon the immutable Word of God, not upon phenomena.

No minister can get results until by preaching the Word of God, he can produce faith for what that Word offers. Sixty thousand churches in the United States reported no conversions in a whole year, but I am not going to offer this fact as a reason for fighting the doctrine of regeneration, or any other part of the Gospel.

Some say, "We believe in healing, but we do not believe in parading it." I have noticed that some who fail to rejoice with those who succeed in receiving healing from Christ, are quick to parade a failure, while saying nothing about the successes. To me, it is a mystery how any Christian can fail to rejoice when a poor afflicted person has been healed by Christ. I not only rejoice when a sufferer has been healed by Christ, but I am glad to parade God's mercy to the world. "Make known His deeds among the people," is the command of God. Jesus commanded the demoniac, out of whom He cast the devil, to go back to his own community and tell what great mercy Christ had shown him, and the Scriptures tell us that "he published throughout Decapolis, this mercy of Christ," and in the next chapter we read of multitudes in Decapolis being healed by Christ; and that the multitudes glorified the God of Israel.

4. *The healing part of the Gospel is hindered and even made void by the traditions of men.*

Jesus said to the Jewish teachers of His day, "Ye have made void the law by your traditions." In our day most preachers have done worse, for they have made void a part of the Gospel by their traditions.

(1) One tradition is *that God is the author of disease* and that He wills the sickness of some of His worshippers. It is a mystery to me how anyone can hold this view in the face of the Scriptures and the ministry of Christ, who for three years healed all that were oppressed of the devil, or, at least, all such as came to Him for healing.

If sickness is the will of God for His worshippers, then every physician is a law-breaker, every trained nurse is defying the Almighty and every hospital is a house of rebellion instead of a house of mercy. If God wants one to be sick, it is a sin for that one even to want to be well, because we are to love the will of God; whatever that will may be.

(2) Another tradition which is responsible for thousands dying a premature death after years of physical agony, is the teaching that *we can glorify God more by remaining sick and exhibiting patience than we can by being divinely healed.* An honest but unenlightened minister will often kneel at the bedside of one suffering with arthritis or cancer or some other dangerous disease and pray, "Lord, since in Thy loving providence Thou hast seen fit to lay Thine afflicting hand upon our dear sister, give her fortitude and patience to bear this affliction." This he does instead of obeying the plain command to anoint "any sick" in the Church and to pray "the prayer of faith" for their healing (James 5:14); which method John Wesley says was the only process of healing in the Church until it was lost through unbelief.

Now, if it is true, as many are taught, that one can glorify God more by remaining sick than by being healed, then Jesus did not hesitate to rob His Father of all the glory He possibly could by healing everyone that appealed to Him for help during His entire earthly ministry. And His successor, the Holy Spirit, who was sent down to augment what Christ had begun to do and to teach, hesitated not to rob God of all the glory He could by healing everyone in the streets of Jerusalem (Acts 5:15, 16), and Paul did not hesitate to rob God of all the glory he could by healing all the other sick on the Island of Melita.

(3) The most common and threadbare tradition is the worn-out statement that "the age of miracles has passed." Of all the present-day "traditions of the elders" or ministers, this is the most foolish, illogical and unscriptural of any that I know. The Holy Spirit, in whose age we are now living, is God's only Miracle Worker, the only Administrator of the Father's will; the One who healed all the sick multitudes who came to Christ for healing during the days of His flesh.

All the miracles ever wrought until the Day of Pentecost were accomplished by the Spirit, the Miracle Worker, before He had entered officially for His own dispensation.

The age in which we live was intended by our Heavenly Father to be the most miraculous of all the dispensations because it is the Miracle Worker's age, the Holy Spirit's dispensation. During this age the great promise is that God will pour out the Holy Spirit, the Miracle Worker, upon all flesh. This is the only age in which the Miracle Worker would incarnate Himself; this is the only age in which the nine gifts of the Spirit—including the gifts of faith, healing and miracles—were to be distributed to every man severally as He, the Holy Spirit, will. Jesus declared that the works which He was doing would be continued and that even "greater works" would be done by the Holy Spirit, the Miracle Worker, after He should have entered office during Christ's exaltation; which is during the Spirit's dispensation.

How absurd and ridiculous for any professed Bible Teacher to pick out this, the Miracle Worker's age, as the only age when miracles are not to be done! How absurd for such an one to teach that the Holy Spirit will work miracles in every age but His own age! which is a "better" dispensation, with "better" priest, "better covenant," "better" promises, and "better" everything, than any previous age.

Some talk as though the present age is not the Holy Spirit's age. There is but one Spirit dispensation, and that one lies between the first and second advents of our Lord. It is true, we are living in the Laodicean or lukewarm period of the Spirit's dispensation. At the beginning of the age the Church was in her Spirit-filled period, and we are now in the luke-warm period of the same age. But, for one (And, thank God! there are many others like me.), I am going to base both my preaching and my practicing on the preaching and the practicing of the Church during her Spirit-filled period, rather than on the preaching and practicing of the Church during her lukewarm peroid. I would rather labor to lift the True Church up to the Bible standard of the first century than to try to make the Bible fit the standard of the lukewarm church of the twentieth century. In previous discourses we have seen that God has worked miracles in each of the centuries since the closing of the Scriptures, down to our day, and that this worn-out tradition which we are considering is entirely set aside by the facts of history.

(4) Another tradition is that *it is not God's will to heal all.* In our book, "Christ the Healer," and in previous discourses over the air, we have answered this objection from every conceivable angle. If it is God's will to heal only some of those who need healing, then none have any basis for faith, until they shall have received a special revelation that they are among the favored ones. If God's promises to heal are not for all, then no man can ascertain the will of God for himself from the Bible. Are we to understand from such teachers that we must close our Bibles and get our revelation directly from the Spirit before we can pray for the sick, because the will of God in this matter cannot be ascertained from the Scriptures? This would be virtually to teach that the whole of the Divine activity on the line of healing would have to be governed by direct revelations from the Spirit instead of by the Scriptures.

(5) Still others are hindered from receiving healing by being taught to add to their prayer for healing the faith-destroying phrase, *"If it be Thy will."* There is only one case given in the New Testament of one asking for healing in this way. That is the case of the leper, who said, "If Thou wilt, Thou canst make me whole." This man could not have prayed otherwise, because he was not yet informed

as to the will of God in the matter. Jesus did not heal this leper until he had added to his faith that Jesus *could* heal him the faith that Jesus *would* heal him. The "I will" of Jesus cancelled the "If" of the leper. It is impossible for one ever to pray with faith until the "If" has been removed from his prayer. To have real faith is to be "fully persuaded" that God will do what He has promised to do, and no one is ever "fully persuaded" when he adds to his prayer, "If it be Thy will." Since God has revealed His will in this matter by His promises, for us to say, "If it be Thy will" when praying for healing is the same as to say, "If it be Thy will to keep Thy promise."

(6) Another unscriptural premise that has sent thousands of sufferers to premature graves and kept multitudes of others from receiving healing, is the modern teaching that *Paul's thorn in the flesh* was some kind of physical trouble. The falsity of this position is shown in the following sermon on "Paul's Thorn in the Flesh."

The expression "thorn in the flesh" is not once used in either the Old or the New Testament except as an illustration. The figure of the "thorn in the flesh" is not in one single instance used in the Bible as a figure of sickness. Every time the phrase is used in the Bible it is specifically stated exactly what the "thorn in the flesh" was. For instances, in Numbers 33:55 Moses told the children of Israel, before they entered the Land of Canaan, "If ye will not drive out the inhabitants of the land from before you; then it shall come to pass, that those which ye let remain of them shall be pricks in your eyes, and thorns in your sides, and shall vex ye in the land wherein ye dwell."

Here the Scripture itself plainly tells us that the "pricks" in the eyes and the "thorns" in the sides of the Israelites were the spared inhabitants of Canaan—not eye trouble or sickness. God was only illustrating to show that as a thorn sticking in the flesh is annoying, so the Canaanites, if allowed to remain in the land, would be a constant annoyance to the Children of Israel. And so in all the other places in the Bible where this expression is used, the thorns are personalities.

As in each of the other instances the Bible definitely states what the thorn was, so in this particular instance Paul as definitely states what his thorn was. He said it was "The messenger (Greek angelos) of Satan," or, as translated by others, "The angel of the devil," "Satan's angel," etc.

The Greek word "angelos" appears one hundred and eighty-eight times in the Bible. It is translated "angel" one hundred and eighty-one times and "messenger" the other seven times. In every one of the one hundred and eighty-eight times where this word is used in the Bible it means a person, not a thing. Hell was made for "the devil and his angels," and an angel or a messenger is always a person that one person sends to another—never a disease.

Paul not only tells us that his thorn was an angel or messenger of Satan, but he also tells us what that angel came to do, viz., "to buffet me," as when "the waves buffeted" the boat, and as when the soldiers "buffeted" Christ. Accordingly Weymouth translates this passage in this way, "Satan's angel dealing blow after blow." Since "buffeting" means giving *repeated* blows, if Paul's buffeting was a physical one, it would have had to be a succession of diseases, or the same disease many times repeated, or he could not have termed it buffeting.

In speaking of this messenger or angel, Rotherham's translation uses the pronoun "he." Weymouth's translation says, "As to this, three times I besought the Lord to rid me of *him*."

These two pronouns, as well as the word "angel" or "messenger," prove that Paul's thorn was, as he himself plainly shows, a Satanic personality—not a disease. Paul could not have used the personal pronouns "he" and "him" when speaking of a disease, because there is no personality to disease. Paul enumerates almost every kind of trouble one can think of as his buffeting, but disease is not on the list.

In doing and so revealing to us the unchanging will of God, Jesus healed every sick person that ever applied to Him for Healing, but did not promise to take away the buffetings or persecution.

Those of you who have listened to our broadcasts have seen that Paul was the most prolific teacher in the Bible on the subject of Divine Healing.

(7) Another tradition that has hindered the ministry of healing is the teaching that *Jesus healed the sick as the Son of God, not as the Son of Man.* Such teachers believe that as we are not Christs we cannot expect such works today. The Scriptures teach us that Jesus, the Son of God, emptied Himself and became like unto His brethren in all things, except as to sin. He speaks of Himself as "The Son of Man" about eighty times, and as the Son of Man He said, "I can of Mine own self do nothing." This certainly was not true of Him before He became the Son of Man, because all things were made by Him and for Him. We have already seen that Jesus did His works in reliance upon the Spirit, and that He "began both to do and teach, until the day He was taken up," what He Himself promised in John 14:12 to continue and augment in answer to the prayers of the Church when He should be glorified. The very words here quoted from Acts 1:1, "Jesus *began* both to do and teach," prove that what the Lord "began" both in *doing* and *teaching* was to be continued by the Holy Spirit operating through the Church.

5. *I assign for the failure of some to receive healing the breaking of natural laws.*

Let it be remembered that natural laws are God's laws and that they are as Divine as are His miracles. Nature is God in action, but not miraculously. Because of their ignorance of natural laws some are not supplying their bodies with the required nourishment, or they may be overeating while asking God to heal them of stomach trouble, and thereby hindering the answer to their prayers. After God had revealed Himself as Jehovah-Rapha—our Healer—the conditions He imposed were that the people observe His laws of health. There are times when sufferers who are ignorant of dietetics and other simple requirements need the advice of some one who is qualified to give advice in such matters.

6. *Some are not healed because of unbelief on the part of the elder or minister who prays for them.*

Christ's disciples, although divinely commissioned to cast out devils and to heal the sick, failed to deliver the epileptic boy. When Jesus came down from the mountain He delivered the boy and rebuked the disciples for their unbelief.

7. *Some are not healed because their affliction is the work of an evil spirit which must be cast out.*

Jesus did not heal the epileptic *disease* but cast out the epileptic *spirit*. He also cast out the deaf and dumb and blind spirits. He says of those who "believe," "In My name they shall cast out demons." Many times we have seen people instantly delivered when we rebuked the afflicting spirit, merely speaking representatively, in Christ's Name, or by His authority.

8. *Some fail to receive healing because they regard iniquity in their heart.*

Such aught to learn to say with David: "If I regard iniquity in my heart, the Lord will not hear me." God has not promised to destroy the works of the devil in the body while we are clinging to the works of the devil in the soul. Unconfessed sin hinders people from receiving God's mercy. His Word tells us, "He that covereth his sins shall not prosper, but whoso confesseth and forsaketh them, shall obtain mercy."

9. *In this Laodicean period of the Church lukewarmness is one of the great hindrances to healing.*

After Christ was glorified He sent down the message, "I would thou wert cold or hot. So then because thou art lukewarm, and neither cold nor hot, I will spue thee out of my mouth."

The best thing for us it to be red hot for God, the next best thing is to be cold, but it is fatal to be lukewarm, for the Lord said He would spue out the lukewarm.

Lukewarmness is a much worse disease than cancer, therefore God wants to heal lukewarmness first. He has promised and is waiting to heal our backsliding and flood our hearts with His love. God says of the man whose heart is "hot" with love for Him, "Because he hath set his love upon Me, therefore will I deliver him." Serving God with gladness and cheerfulness of heart was the condition for healing in Old Testament times. Surely the standard ought not be lowered in this day of grace!

10. *Sickness and affliction are permitted to remain on some as a halter, with which God leads them into the center of His will, and when this has been done, He removes the halter.*

If God were to take the halter off too soon, many would run away, and so would deprive themselves of the pleasure of living out the Divine program. It is impossible to pray "the prayer of faith" to get the halter off from those who are unwilling to be led into the glorious center of God's will.

11. *An unforgiving spirit, or holding a grudge, hinders some from receiving the Lord's healing.*

Jesus said, "If ye forgive not men their trespasses, neither will your Heavenly Father forgive your trespasses."

The first thing we need and the first thing God wants to grant us is the forgiveness of our sins, but God cannot forgive us when we will not forgive others. And if He cannot forgive us He certainly cannot heal us. Many times we have seen the afflicted healed "in the twinkling of an eye" when they were ready to forgive those who had wronged them.

12. *Wrongs unrighted hinder the faith of some to receive healing.*

Those who have wronged their neighbor in any way must ask his forgiveness. We have known many who, terribly afflicted, were healed as soon as this was done.

13. *Some have no purpose and no diligence when seeking God for healing.*

God "is the rewarder of them that *diligently* seek Him." We have known sufferers to undergo as many as a dozen or more operations without any positive promise of being healed. Yet in coming to God for healing, which He positively promises to give, many do not come with anything like the diligence shown by those who apply for help from man.

14. *Because of not being properly instructed, many fail to be healed because they endeavor to confine God to miracles.*

Because they are not made well and strong in an instant, these people cast away their confidence.

God differentiates between a miracle and a healing. If every man, wasted with disease, were made strong and well in a moment, there would be no healings, for they would all be miracles. When enumerating the spiritual gifts, Paul speaks of gifts of healing and also of miracles. Christ could do no miracle in Nazareth because of the unbelief of the people there, but He did heal a few sick folk there. Confusing healings with miracles is a very common hindrance to healing in these days, when there is so little clear teaching on the subject.

15. *Some wax weak in faith by watching their symptoms.*

Instead of doing this they, like Abraham of old, should be waxing strong in faith by looking unto the promise of God. These people make their feelings the basis for faith rather than God's Word, which He has made its only basis.

16. *Others fail to receive healing because they do not act their faith.*

"Faith without works is dead." It is not God's turn to move until we have faith with corresponding actions. The literal translation of Mark 11:22—"Have faith in God"— is *"Reckon on God's faithfulness."*

The full exercise of faith means that we *think* faith, *speak* faith, *act* faith. To the blind man, Jesus said, "Go, wash in the Pool of Siloam." This act gave the man an opportunity to exercise faith in heart, mind and body. He was not healed until he had first given this visible expression of his faith. He believed the healing was his *before* it was manifested.

It was the same with Naaman, the leper, and also with the ten lepers to whom Jesus said, "Go, shew yourselves to the priests." The record is, "As they went, they were cleansed." A *visible expression* of faith, including their heart, mind and body, was required *before* their healing was manifested. Some miss being healed by reversing this Divine order.

17. *Others when tested, cast away their confidence, failing to see that, as with Abraham, by the test their faith should be perfected, not destroyed.*

We are made partakers on the condition that we hold the beginning of our confidence steadfast unto the end (Heb. 10:35). If the Word of God is the reason for our faith, then it is never right to cast away our confidence in it.

18. *Some fail to receive healing by neglecting to receive the Holy Spirit, who has been sent to impart to us the blessings of redemption.*

In Romans 8:11 Paul tells us that our mortal [not actually although judicially dead] bodies [also] are to be quickened by the Spirit that dwelleth *in* [not outside of] us. Since our bodies are the temples of the Holy Ghost, and the Holy Ghost applies the healing, we might say that He is the Carpenter who repairs the house. Some are consciously keeping the Carpenter outside of the house while asking Him to repair it on the inside. Paul said, "The body for the Lord" before he said, "The Lord for the body." We must present our bodies a living sacrifice (Rom. 12:1), and let them become the temples of the Holy Ghost if we want them healed. This reason for failure does not usually apply to those who are untaught as to their privilege of being filled with the Spirit.

19. *Some are not healed because they substitute their belief in the doctrine of Divine Healing for personal faith to be healed.*

20. *Some are not healed because of their failure to receive the written promise of God as His direct Word to them.*

They fail to recognize that to faith the Word of God is the Voice of God. In Psalm 138:2 we read, "Thou hast magnified Thy Word above all Thy Name."

21. *Some will not believe that their prayer for healing has been heard until they have experienced and seen the answer.*

Christ has not promised that our healing shall begin before we believe that He has heard our prayer. Some suppose that they must keep on praying and not believe that their prayer has been heard, until they are well. This is exactly the opposite of what God requires.

In Mark 11:24 Jesus tells us exactly the conditions He requires for our appropriation of the blessings He has promised. He says, "What things soever ye desire, *when ye pray,* believe that ye receive them, and ye shall have them." That is, "ye shall have them" *after* you believe He has heard your prayer. As Jesus said, "I thank Thee that Thou *hast* heard Me," while Lazarus was still dead; so we should be able to say, "I thank Thee that Thou *hast* heard me," while we are still sick. "Ye shall have them," is your answer from Jesus, and it is also your proof that your prayer has been heard.

As we have already remarked, to faith the Word of God is the Voice of God. God has not promised that our healing shall begin before we believe that He has heard our prayer. "If we ask anything according to His will, He heareth us." If this is true, then we must believe that our prayer has been heard when we really pray. We must be able to say, "We know we have the petition that we desire of Him," not because we see the answer, but because "God is faithful, who also will do it."

Abraham did not keep on praying for the birth of Isaac until the child was born. Instead, he kept on believing and glorifying God for His Word in the matter.

More than once we have read that it was *after* Solomon had "made an end of praying" that the blessing came.

Jesus, at the grave of Lazarus, had "made an end of praying," and had said, "I thank Thee that Thou hast heard Me," before Lazarus came out from his tomb.

Jehoshaphat and the children of Israel had "made an end of praying" and were all praising God "with a loud voice" for the answer to their prayers before they went out to do battle with the three great armies. Their faith was "the evidence [or assurance] of things not [yet] seen." Heb. 11:1.

The one hundred and twenty had "made an end of praying" and were all "continually praising and blessing God" when the Spirit was poured out upon them.

It is supposed to be the "end of praying" when one has been anointed for healing, and if one who has been anointed really has fatih, we will hear nothing from him but thanksgiving until he has been healed.

When a child teases her mother for a new dress until the mother says, "I will get it for you," the child makes an end of teasing before there is any dress in sight. Instead of continuing to say, "Please give me a dress," she says, "Goody! Goody!"

Perhaps I should say here that after commitment, one must not become indifferent. One's trust must remain active, like that of the Children of Israel when they marched around the walls of Jericho and blew their rams' horns; and like that of Jehoshaphat and his men who, after they had "made an end of praying," went out to battle, singing praises to God.

The healing of the ten lepers came while their trust was still active.

God said to the dying Israelites, "Every one that *looketh* shall live." This word "looketh" is in the continuous present tense. It is not a mere glance, but a continuous "stare."

"Moses endured by *seeing* [continuously seeing] Him who is invisible."

It was a *"steadfast"* faith that brought the fulfillment of God's promise to Abraham. Abraham waxed strong in faith by *looking* [continuously] unto the promise of God.

If we allow our trust to become inactive, it will weaken; if we keep it active, it will continually grow stronger.

22. *Some hinder God by basing their faith on their improvement after prayer rather than upon His promise.*

They do not realize that there is no other reason for faith as good as the Word of God, and that God wants to train every Christian to believe Him when everything they can see, except His promise, is to the contrary. Amen, and Amen!

14

Paul's Thorn

"And lest I should be exalted above measure through the abundance of the revelations, there was given me a thorn in the flesh, the messenger of Satan to buffet me, lest I should be exalted above measure. For this thing I besought the Lord thrice, that it might depart from me. And He said unto me, My grace is sufficient for thee: for my strength is made perfect in weakness. Most gladly therefore will I rather glory in my infirmities, that the power of Christ may rest upon me. Therefore I take pleasure in infirmities, in reproaches, in necessities, in persecutions, in distresses for Christ's sake: for when I am weak, then am I strong" (II Cor. 12:7-10).

One of the most prevalent objections raised today against the ministry of healing is Paul's "thorn in the flesh." One traditional idea has led to another. The widespread teaching that God is the Author of disease, and that some of the most devout of His children He has desired shall remain sick, and glorify Him by exhibiting fortitude and patience, no doubt has led to the idea that Paul had a sickness that God refused to heal. We do not believe that any one who would take time to read all that God has to say on the subject of healing could ever form such a conclusion.

I am quick to admit that equally devout men may hold contrary views, not only on this point, but on the whole subject of Divine healing. It is merely a matter of study and investigation. Many good men whose teaching has been that the age of miracles is past, etc., while reading the Scriptures, have thoughtlessly passed over the Bible teaching on healing, believing it not applicable for our day. Nearly all who have spoken and written against us have not hesitated to use our name, and "go after us with hammer and tongs"; but they never have attempted to answer the scriptural arguments that we have presented in our sermons on the subject. We have carefully, without mentioning their names, read their statements publicly and answered them from the Scriptures. If we were fighting against "flesh and blood" we would name them, and "go after them with a vengeance," but this would not be Christ-like. We feel disposed to "keep our hands off" God's servants, and let Him fight our battles for us.

A Clergyman's Absurd Exposition

Before considering the subject of Paul's "thorn," we quote the following from a stenographic report of a sermon preached by a prominent New York clergyman, and which he also revised, printed in great quantities, and distributed in every home in the vicinity of our revival, in order to offset our teaching on healing, of which he had practically no knowledge, having never seen or heard us. Among other things he said:

The fact is—Paul was sick. He was the sickest of men. He had one of the worst and most painful of oriental diseases. He had opthalmia—a disease of the eyes. The proof that he had it is overwhelming. He tells us that he had a "thorn in the flesh." . . . When Paul stood before them his eyes filled with unspeakable pus—unspeakable-looking matter running down over his face . . . Why would they have digged out their eyes for him except that his eyes, as he stood before them, were a pitiable and appealing sight to them—as the eyes of any one with opthalmia are? The particular pain of this disease is that it is like a "stake" in the eyes . . . It is beyond dispute that Paul was a sick man. He says so himself. Paul did not get this disease by infection. How did he get it? Jesus Christ gave it to him. Paul did not want to be sick. He prayed the Lord to heal him from this sickness. He prayed not once, nor twice, but three times. He received no answer to his prayers. In spite of all his praying he got no healing. His thrice-offered prayer brought him no cure, not even the hint of healing. That is not all. The Lord said to Paul a very startling thing. He said, "My grace is sufficient for thee." . . . He tells Paul it is better for him to be sick than to be well. He tells Paul it is the Divine will he shall not be cured . . . He tells Paul Divine power can and will operate in and through him better with opthalmia and sickness than without it . . . Hear what Paul has to say in response to the Lord concerning his infirmity and the will of the Lord that he shall not be cured of it. These are his words, "Most gladly therefore will I rather glory in my infirmity that the Power of Christ may rest upon me." Here is Paul saying just this, "I will glory in my opthalmia. My eyes may be full of repulsive discharges; I may be the object of pity; no matter, I will glory in it. I will rejoice in my sickness." . . . In the quivering flesh and painful suffering of His apostle, the Lord has written His Divine protest against this unspeakable doctrine, this *brutal* transmutation of the cross of Christ into a center of physical healing.

In answering our brother's arguments on this point, we will state, first, that the expression "thorn in the flesh" is not once used in either the Old or New Testaments except as an illustration. The figure of the thorn in the flesh is not in one single instance used in the Bible as a figure of sickness. Every time the expression is used in the entire Bible, it is specifically stated exactly what the "thorn in the flesh" was, as we shall see. For instance, in Numbers 33:55, Moses told the children of Israel, before they entered the Land of Canaan, "If ye will not drive out the inhabitants of the land from before you; then it shall come to pass, that those which ye let remain of them shall be pricks in your eyes and thorns in your sides, and shall vex you in the land wherein ye dwell."

Here the Scripture itself plainly tells us that the "pricks" in the *eyes,* and the "thorns" in the *sides* of the Israelites were the inhabitants of Canaan, and not eye trouble or sickness. These teachers contend that Paul's "thorn" *must* have been a bodily affliction, because Paul says that the "thorn" was "in the *flesh.*" I answer that, in the case of these Israelites, the Scripture says, "pricks in your *eyes,*" and "thorns in your *sides,*" but this does not mean that God was to stick Canaanites in their eyes and sides, with their heels dangling outside. God was only illustrating, to show that, as a thorn sticking in the flesh is annoying, so the Canaanites would, if left remaining, be a constant annoyance to the children of Israel.

The Canaanites a Thorn to Israel

Again, Joshua, eight years later, says, in the 23rd chapter, concerning the heathen nations in Canaan, "they shall be *scourges* in your *sides,* and *thorns* in your *eyes.* So, we see again that the "scourges in their *sides* and thorn in their *eyes*" were Canaanites, and not sore eyes or sore sides. It is here again, as in all other instances, plainly stated what the "thorn" was.

Among the last words of David we read, "the sons of Belial shall be all of them as thorns." Without an exception, in all these cases, the "thorns" are personalities. As in each of these instances it definitely states what the "thorn" was; so Paul definitely states what *his* "thorn" was. He says it was "the messenger (Gr., *Angelos*) of Satan"; or, as translated by others, "the angel of the devil," "Satan's angel," etc.

This Greek word *angelos* appears 188 times in the Bible, and is translated "angel" 181 times, and "messenger" the other seven times. In all the 188 times in the entire Bible, it is in every case a *person* and not a thing—without a solitary exception. "Hell was made for the devil and his angels" (or "messengers,") and an "angel" or a "messenger" is always a *person* that one person sends to another, and never a disease.

Paul's Thorn an Angel of Satan

Paul not only tells us that his "thorn" was an angel of Satan, but he also tells us what the angel came to do: "to buffet me," or, as Rotherham translates it, "that *he* might be buffeting me." Now the word "buffet" means *"blow after blow,"* as when the waves buffeted the boat, and as when they "buffeted" Christ! Accordingly, Weymouth translates "Satan's angel dealing *blow after blow."* Since buffeting means *repeated* blows, if Paul's buffeting was a disease, it would have had to have been many diseases or the same disease many times repeated, to be called buffeting.

In speaking of this messenger, or angel, Rotherham's translation uses the pronoun "he," and Weymouth's translation states, "As for this, three times I besought the Lord to rid me of *him."* Both of these translators use personal pronouns; viz., "he" and "him" when speaking of Paul's thorn; so these two pronouns, as well as the word "angel," or "messenger," prove that Paul's "thorn" was, as he himself plainly shows, a satanic personality and not a disease. We could not use the personal pronouns "he" or "him" when speaking of ophthalmia, or any other disease, because there is no sex to ophthalmia. Suppose I should ask a man how his cancer was, what would you think if you heard him reply, *"Him* is lots worse, and I am suffering terribly." Now since Paul distinctly states that his "thorn" was the angel of Satan sent to buffet him—a demon spirit sent from Satan to make trouble for him wherever he went— why should *we* say it was something else?

Paul's Sufferings

Soon after Paul's conversion, God said to Ananias, "I will show him how great things he must suffer for My name's sake," not by sickness, but by the persecutions which Paul enumerates as his buffetings. Paul had persecuted the Christians from place to place, and now he, himself, was beginning to experience the same and greater persecutions. Specifying the buffetings instigated by Satan's angel, Paul goes on to say, "Therefore I take pleasure in infirmities, in reproaches, in necessities, in persecutions, in distresses for Christ's sake; for when I am weak then am I strong." Paul first mentions "infirmities," for he realized, and every christian should realize, his weakness and inability in his own strength to stand up against a satanic messenger, and to pass triumphantly through "reproaches, necessities, persecutions, distresses," and all the other buffetings he elsewhere catalogues; and this is why he besought the Lord three times to be rid of *"him"* (the messenger) who was buffeting him so severely and in so many ways. Christ responded to his thrice-repeated prayer, not by removing the satanic messenger, but by saying, "My grace (which is for the "inner" man) is sufficient for thee; for My strength is made perfect in weakness."

When Paul saw that the grace of God was sufficient to strengthen him to bear all these things, he exclaimed, "Therefore will I rather glory in my infirmities (weaknesses) that the power of Christ may rest upon me . . . for when I am weak then am I strong." How could it be true that Christ's strength was made perfect in Paul's weakness if he was left weak, or unless Paul was an actual partaker of Christ's strength, which would remove the weakness, whether it was

physical or spiritual? Without God's strength being imparted to him is a man powerful when he is weak, either
physically or spiritually? Paul saw that the grace of God
given him made his very buffetings, even his imprisonments,
to work together for his good and to turn out for the "fur-
therance of the Gospel." What servant of God has not
learned, and probably more than once, that it is when he
is most conscious of his own weakness that the power of
Christ rests upon him the most; or, that it is when he is con-
ciously weakest in himself that he is the strongest because
of depending, not on his own, but on Divine strength?

Grace for Spiritual, not Physical, Infirmities

Paul is clear in teaching that it is the *"Life of Jesus"*
which is "made manifest in our mortal flesh," but it is no-
where stated in the Scriptures that God gives *grace* to our
bodies. The very word "grace" shows that it was the "inner
man" that needed help, because the grace of God is imparted
only to the "inner man," which Paul says, in his case, was
"renewed day by day." In other words, "grace" is for spiritual
infirmities, and not for physical.

While the terms in the Old Testament "pricks in your
eyes and thorns in your sides," were used, the Canaanites
were not an annoyance to the Israelites in the sense of inflicting any physical disease or infirmities upon their bodies.
As the annoying Canaanites were outside the bodies of
the Israelites, so Satan's angel was outside of Paul's body;
for surely the Apostle had no demon inhabiting his body.
God's grace and mercy have always been given to enable
us to bear our persecutions and temptations; but not to bear
our sins and sicknesses, which He bore for us. God has never
promised to take away from christians their *external* buffetings, afflictions and temptations; he gives us grace to bear

them. But throughout history He has ever been ready to take away the *internal,* or bodily, oppressions of the devil, as well as our sins.

For God Was with Him

Jesus "went about doing good, and healing *all* that were oppressed of the devil, for God was with Him." God tells us, "They that will live godly in this present world shall suffer *persecution,*" but He has never said, "They shall remain *sick,*" according to unscriptural views held by many today. This view denies all scriptural precedent. No doubt Paul got the expression "thorn if the flesh" from reading the Old Testament Scriptures, and because the term illustrated their external and not their bodily annoyances, he used the same expression to illustrate his own buffetings.

If the infirmities (weaknesses) of which Paul here speaks, *were* physical, and, according to the above-quoted writer Paul was "the sickest of men," and God would not remove the "thorn" by giving him strength, how could he labor "more abundantly than they all?" If "the sickest of men" can accomplish more work than a well man, then let us all pray for sickness in order that *we* also may do more work for God. After realizing that God's strength was "made perfect in (his) weakness," then Paul could take pleasure, not only in his infirmities, but also in the buffetings which he mentions, reproaches, necessities, persecutions, distresses, etc. Note, here, among other things, that Paul mentions necessities, meaning his financial buffetings, which he also refers to in his first letter to the Corinthians written a year before. He says, "Even unto this present hour, we both hunger and thirst, and are naked, and are *buffeted,* and have no certain dwelling place" (I Cor. 4:11), showing that Paul's idea of buffetings was not a permanent sickness.

Paul Enumerates His Buffetings

If Paul's "thorn" was ophthalmia, or sore eyes, which he does not mention, instead of these reproaches, etc., which he *does* mention why does he not say he takes pleasure in the former instead of in the latter? Not only here, but elsewhere in his letter to the Corinthians, Paul enumerates in detail his buffetings instigated by Satan's angel. In addition to the reproaches, necessities, persecutions and distresses mentioned in our text, in the sixth chapter of this same letter he mentions stripes, imprisonments, tumults, labors, watchings, fastings, dishonor, evil report, deceivers, "as dying and behold we live," "as chastened and not killed," "as sorrowful yet always rejoicing," "as poor yet making many rich," "as having nothing yet possessing all things"; and in the 11th chapter, "stripes above measure, in prisons more frequent, in deaths oft. Of the Jews five times received I forty stripes save one; thrice was I beaten with rods; once was I stoned; thrice I suffered shipwreck . . . a day and a night in the deep; in journeyings often, in perils of waters, in perils of robbers, in perils of mine own countrymen, in perils by the heathen, in perils in the city, in perils in the wilderness, in perils in the sea, in perils among false brethren; in weariness and painfulness, in watchings often, in hunger and thirst: in fastings often, in cold and nakedness." "Reviled . . . persecuted . . . defamed . . . made as the filth of the world . . . the offscouring of all things unto this day."

Questions Worth Considering

Who but Satan's angel could be responsible for all these sufferings? In enumerating them we see that Paul mentions almost everything that one could think of *except* sickness, or ophthalmia. The one thing which he does not mention, and which is conspicuous for its absence, tradition seizes upon and says this was his "thorn." Why do these opposers substitute "sore eyes" or "sickness," neither of which Paul mentions, for all of these buffetings which he *does* mention?

Although it is believed by many good men, one writer remarks that this widespread perversion of the Scriptures dealing with Paul's "thorn in the flesh" is certainly inspired by Satan, because it gives him the privilege of carrying on his evil work of afflicting and tormenting the bodies of humanity.

Since healing is an essential element of the Gospel, how could Paul enjoy "the fulness of the blessing of the Gospel" as he did, and remain sick? Is not healing a part of the blessing of the Gospel? Even such conservative scholars as those constituting the Episcopalian Commission on Healing agree that "bodily healing is an essential element of the Gospel."

Suppose our brother is correct in stating that Paul was the "sickest of men," suffering with ophthalmia, is it not strange that when the Ephesians saw the pus running from Paul's eyes and found that God would not heal him, this sight gave them faith for "special miracles" to be wrought in their behalf? for it is stated here that "God wrought special miracles by the hands of Paul, so that from his body were brought unto the sick handkerchiefs and aprons, and the diseases departed from them, and the evil spirits went out" (Acts 19:11, 12). The Scriptures never speak of special miracles in connection with any but this "sickest" Apostle. Today, if handkerchiefs were brought from one suffering with ophthalmia, rather than laying them on the sick for healing, we would burn them to keep from spreading the infection.

The Case of the Cripple at Lystra

Again, when the heathen cripple at Lystra heard Paul preach "the Gospel," and got a glimpse of Paul's eyes, with their "repulsive discharges," (?) the sight at once gave him faith to walk for the first time on earth, and Paul "perceiving that he had faith to be healed, said with a loud voice, 'stand upright on thy feet,' and he leaped and walked." This heathen cripple had never witnessed a miracle nor ever heard the Gospel preached until he heard it from "the sickest of men" whom God wills "shall not be cured."

Again, is it not marvelous how Paul, with "unspeakable pus—unspeakable-looking matter running down over his face," "the sickest of men," suffering with the "worst and most painful of oriental diseases . . . a pitiable and appealing sight to them," and "Jesus Christ gave it to him," telling him, "it is the Divine will he shall not be cured"—I say is it not marvelous how Paul in this condition could "make the *Gentiles* obedient by word and deed *through mighty signs and wonders,* by the power of the Spirit of God, . . . from Jerusalem round about unto Illyricum?" (Rom. 15:18, 19).

Again, on the island of Melita, after seeing Paul's unsightly disease, which must remain because "Divine power can and will operate in and through him better with ophthalmia and sickness than without it," first, the father of Publius and then "all the other sick people in the island came and were cured" (Acts 28:8, 9—Weymouth).

Do the Sick Glory in Sickness?

The brother above quoted says, "Paul is saying just this, 'I will glory in my opthalmia; my eyes may be full of repulsive discharges; I may be the object of pity; no matter, I will glory in it. I will rejoice in my sickness!' " Since these men teach it is right for Paul to glory in his being "the sickest of men," why do they not also glory in *their* sickness instead of doing their best to be rid of it? If they glory in their "thorn," why have some of them gone to a surgeon to have it cut out?

Some teachers hold that Paul's "thorn" was a partial blindness caused by the brightness of the Divine light that shone upon him at his conversion. He, himself, tells us, in the year 60, when he wrote this epistle, that it was "above 14 years ago" that he received the abundance of the revelations which occasioned the giving of the "thorn in the flesh"; making it 12 years after his conversion that the "thorn" was given, this epistle having been written 26 years after his conversion. And, again, it would be well nigh blasphemy to speak of a partial blindness caused by a personal glimpse of the glorified Christ as "the messenger of Satan."

Why Paul's "Thorn"?

Paul distinctly states that his buffeting by the messenger was given him lest he should be "exalted above measure through *the abundance of the revelations.*" Is it because of the abundance of their revelations that the sick everywhere today must be taught to regard their sickness as a "thorn," which must remain lest *they* be exalted?

Since Paul's "thorn" was no hindrance to *his* faith for the healing of *"all* the other sick people in the island" of Melita, and elsewhere, why should it hinder *ours;* or why *should* it be taught today everywhere as a hindrance to what little faith for healing the sick may have received? The Bible says, "faith *cometh* by hearing," but in these days faith *leaveth* by hearing—hearing these foolish doctrines. The widespread error concerning Paul's "thorn in the flesh" severs the Gospel, and entirely removes the foundation upon which faith for healing must rest unless the sick one received, from the Spirit and *not from the Bible,* a special revelation that he is to be healed.

We have noticed from the writings of these teachers that they are quick to mention the slightest physical defect in those who teach healing and are seeing the sick healed, and yet they argue that it was proper for Paul, who is the most outstanding New Testament teacher of healing, to have, as they contend, the "thorn" of bodily affliction. If we could duplicate Paul's wonderful ministry of healing while "unspeakable pus" was all the time running from *our* eyes, would not this be seized upon by these very teachers as a ground for ridicule?

Paul's Thorn not a Hindrance to Labor

The Scriptures show that Paul's "thorn" did not hinder him from laboring more abundantly than all others, but those who are taught that their sickness is a "thorn" that must remain are often incapacitated by *their* "thorn" /from *any* labor, not even being able to care for themselves, but increasing other people's labors by having to be waited upon. It was the Apostle Paul who wrote that we may be "prepared unto every good work," "thoroughly furnished unto all good works," "zealous of good works," "careful to maintain good works," and "perfect in every good work to do His will." How can the multitude of christians confined to their sickrooms by a "thorn in the flesh" "abound unto every good work?" Do these several Scriptures belong only to well christians?

If Christ's words "My grace is sufficient" mean that He is telling Paul to remain sick, it would be the first and only instance in the Bible in which God ever told any one to keep his disease; and then the very fact of it being a solitary exception would prove the rule, and what the Scriptures abundantly show, that He healed all others. Why do so many of these teachers today reverse the Scriptures, and make Paul's "thorn" the prominent point when discussing healing, and keep in the background the universal policy of healing revealed throughout the history recorded in the Bible? Paul's "thorn" did not hinder him from finishing his course for God (II Tim. 4:7), while present-day teaching concerning Paul's "thorn" has sent multitudes, often after many years of terrible suffering, to premature graves, with their course only half run — a constantly recurring, and horrible, tragedy!

Paul's Praying a Worthy Example

If the afflicted who believe this latter day teaching will follow Paul by praying until God speaks to them and tells them, as they think He did Paul, that He wants them to keep their affliction, and gives them the reason for it, we would quickly say, "Amen!" for we love the will of God.

In Gal. 4:13, Paul does say, "Ye know how through infirmity of the flesh I preached the Gospel unto you *at the first*." Probably the infirmtiy here was physical, but "at the first" does not mean that he remained weak. Does it not mean the opposite? Else why would he say "at the first?" Probably, as some scholars believe, this was just after his stoning at Lystra.

After Paul, in the plainest words, tells what his "thorn" was, how strange that ministers today should say it is something else, and use it against the scriptural doctrine of healing, when Paul, himself, was the greatest teacher on this subject among the apostles and other writers of the New Testament.

Paul's Preaching Stimulative of Faith

For instance, it was the gospel Paul preached in Ephesus that gave faith for the "special miracles" of healing we have mentioned. He said, concerning his own preaching there, "I have kept back nothing that was profitable for you." If all preachers today would keep back nothing that was profitable, they would surely all be teaching healing.

In Romans 15:18-20, it was Paul who said he "fully preached the Gospel of Christ (preached the full Gospel), and made the Gentiles obedient by word and deed through mighty signs and wonders by the power of the Spirit of God . . . from Jerusalem round about unto Illyricum."

Twenty-five years after he had become an Apostle, he wrote to the Corinthians (I Cor. 11:30), "For this cause many are weak and sickly among you." If Paul's "thorn" was physical infirmity, or he was sick, they would probably write back to him asking, "For what cause are *you* weak and sickly?"

It was Paul who wrote, "Know ye not that your bodies are the temples of the Holy Ghost?" "the members of Christ;" "members of His body, of His flesh, and of His bones;" that "we have the firstfruits of the Spirit" (firstfruits of our spiritual and physical salvation), "that the life also of Jesus might be made manifest in our . . . mortal flesh" (II Cor. 4:11); that "the Spirit . . . shall also quicken your *mortal* (not dead) bodies" (Romans 8:11); that "He is the Savior of the body,"--"The Lord for the body and the body for the Lord."

Called To Be Saints

Paul is the Apostle who wrote "Unto the Church of God which is at Corinth . . . called to be saints, with all that in *every place* call upon the name of Jesus Christ our Lord . . . God hath set some in the Church . . . miracles

. . . gifts of healing," etc.; that these "gifts and callings of
God are without repentance" (i.e., are not revoked); and
that all are commanded to "covet earnestly the best gifts."

Paul did not believe, as men are teaching today, that
these blessings were confined to Israel, but he did believe
that the "middle wall of partition" was "broken down,"
that in Christ there is "neither Jew nor Greek," but that
we are "all one in Christ Jesus." Accordingly, he heals the
Gentile at Lystra crippled from birth, the same as Peter and
John did the *Jewish* cripple at the Beautiful Gate. Paul
also believed that the Old Testament types "were written
for our admonition;" that "as many as are of faith are
Abraham's seed;" that "to Abraham and his seed were the
promises made;" and that "if ye be Christ's then are ye
Abraham's seed, and heirs according to the promise" (Gal.
3:29).

Paul on the Island of Melita

It was Paul who taught that it was "in Him that "all
the promises of God . . . are yea and amen," "to the glory
of God by *us*." In other words, that all the promises of
God, including all His promises to heal, owe their existence
and power to the substitutionary work of Christ for us;
that the redeeming work of Christ was for *all;* and, accordingly, the very last chapter of Acts shows us that Paul believed
and proved that it was God's will to heal, not some of them,
but "all the other sick people in the island" of Melita
(Acts 28:9, Weymouth).

Paul differentiated between miracles and healing, and
therefore did not believe in *every* person being instantly
made whole, because he left Trophimus at Miletum sick,
and Epaphroditus was "sick nigh unto death" for the Gospel's
sake (or from overwork), and from which he did not re-

cover instantneously. Paul was not a fanatic concerning the natural laws of health, which are as Divine as God's miracles, and he did not hesitate to recommend "the fruit of the vine" in the place of water alone for Timothy's stomach trouble.

Paul believed in the sick themselves having faith for healing, for he did not say to the cripple "stand upright on thy feet," until he perceived that "he had faith to be healed." Jesus, Himself, could do no miracle in Nazareth because of community unbelief.

An Instructive Resume

Is it not strange how any minister can set aside the whole Bible, as far as the subject of healing is concerned, keeping in the background—

God's Redemptive and Covenant name, "Jehovah-Rapha," God's Covenant of Healing,

The teaching and promises of healing in the Old Testament types,

The universal precedent of healing set throughout the history of the Old Testament,

The words, teaching, commands, promises, and healing ministry of Christ, by which He revealed the will of God for our bodies,

The gifts of healing set in the Church,

The Church ordinance of anointing, which is commanded,

The fact that Christ bore our sicknesses as well as our sins on Calvary,

The multiplied thousands of those healed since the days of the Apostles, down to and including our days in particular.

Is it not strange that they can set all of this aside, and, when speaking on the subject of healing, choose as their text the Scripture concerning Paul's "thorn," which scholars admit they cannot prove has any reference to either sickness or healing?

Thirty-One Questions

Propounded by Evangelist F. F. Bosworth in the Alliance
Tabernacle, Toronto, Canada, April 20, 1923, As a Part
of His Sermon Answering the Question of an Opposer, "Is
There a Gospel of Healing?"

1. Since the seven compound names of Jehovah, one of
which Jehovah-Rapha (I am the Lord that healeth thee)
reveal His redemptive relationship toward each person, do
they not point to Calvary?
2. Since all the promises of God are yea and amen in
Him do not these seven names including Jehovah-Rapha
(the Lord our Healer) owe their existence and their power
to the redeeming work of Christ on the cross?
3. Has not every believer the same redemptive right to
call upon Christ as Jehovah-Rapha (the Healer of his body)
as he has to call upon Him as Jehovah-Tsidkenu (the Healer
of his soul)? Is not His name given for healing as long as
it is for salvation?
4. If bodily healing is to be obtained independent of Calvary, as opposers teach, why was it that no blessing of the
Year of Jubilee was to be announced by the sounding of
the trumpet until the Day of Atonement?
5. If healing for the body was not a part of Christ's redeeming work, why were types of the Atonement given in
connection with healing throughout the Old Testament?
6. If healing was not in the Atonement why were the
dying Israelites required to look at the type of the Atonement

207

for bodily healing? If both forgiveness and healing came by a look at the type, why not from the antitype?

7. Since their curse was removed by the lifting up of the type of Christ was not our curse of disease also removed by the lifting up of Christ Himself? (Galatians 3:13).

8. In the passage, "Surely He hath borne our sicknesses and carried our pains" (Isaiah 53:4) why are the same Hebrew verbs for "borne" and "carried" employed as are used in verses 11 and 12 for the substitutionary bearing of sin unless they have the same substitutionary and expiatory character?

9. If healing was not provided for all in redemption, how did the multitudes obtain from Christ what God did not provide?

10. If the body was not included in redemption, how can there be a resurrection or how can corruption put on incorruption or mortality put on immortality? Were not the physical as well as the spiritual earnests (foretastes) of our coming redemption enjoyed by God's people throughout history?

11. Why should not the "Last Adam" take away all that the first Adam brought upon us?

12. Since the Church is the body of Christ does God want the body of Christ sick? Is it not His will to heal any part of the body of Christ? If not, why does He command "any sick" in it to be anointed for healing?

13. Are human imperfections of any sort, be they physical or moral, God's will or are they man's mistakes?

14. Since "the body is for the Lord, a living sacrifice unto God" would He not rather have a well body than a wrecked one? If not, how can He make us "perfect in every good work to do His will" or have us "thoroughly furnished unto every good work?"

15. Since bodily healing in the New Testament was called a mercy and it was mercy and compassion that moved Jesus to heal all who came to Him, is not the promise of God still true, "He is plenteous in Mercy unto all that call upon Him?"

16. Does not the glorious Gospel dispensation offer as much mercy and compassion to its sufferers as did the darker dispensations? If not, why would God withdraw this mercy and this Old Testament privilege from a better dispensation with its "better Covenant?"

17. If as some teach, God has another method for our healing today, why would God adopt a less successful method for our better dispensation?

18. Since Christ came to do the Father's will, was not the universal healing of all the sick who came to Him, a revelation of the will of God for our bodies?

19. Did not Jesus emphatically say that He would continue His same works in answer to our prayers while He is with the Father (John 14:12-13) and is not this promise alone a complete answer to all opposers?

20. Why would the Holy Spirit who healed all the sick before His dispensation began, do less after He entered into office on the day of Pentecost? Or did the Miracle-Worker enter office to do away with miracles?

21. Is not the book of the Acts of the Holy Ghost a revelation of the way He wants to continue to act through the Church?

22. How can God justify us and at the same time require us to remain under the curse of the law which Jesus redeemed us from by bearing it for us on the cross? (Gal. 3:13).

23. Since "The Son of God was manifested that He might destroy the works of the devil" has He now relinquished

this purpose which He retained even during the bloody sweat of Gethsemane and the tortures of Calvary? Or does He now want the works of the devil in our bodies to continue that He formerly wanted to destroy? Does God want a cancer,—"a plague," "a curse"—"the works of the devil" in the members of Christ? "Know ye not that your bodies are the members of Christ?" (Cor. 6:15) .

24. Are the proofs of Divine Healing among the one hundred and eighty-four persons who testified in this Tabernacle the last two Friday nights, less bright and convincing than the proofs of Spiritual Redemption among professed Christians today?

Are not these 184 who have been healed in better health physically than a like number of professed Christians are spiritually?

Would not the physical health of these 184 compare favorably with the spiritual health of even the same number of ministers of our day?

25. Would not the argument commonly employed against Divine Healing, drawn from its failures, if employed against justification, regeneration and all the rest be simply overwhelming?

26. Does the fact that Christ could do no miracle at Nazareth prove anything except the unbelief of the people or would it be right to conclude, because of the failure of Christ's disciples to cast out the epileptic spirit from the boy, that it was not God's will to deliver him? Christ proved by healing him that it is God's will to heal even those who fail to receive it.

27. Is not God as willing to show the mercy of healing to His worshippers as He is to show the mercy of forgiveness to His enemies? (Rom. 8:32) .

28. If Paul (as a New York minister says) "was the sickest of men suffering from ophthalmia of the eyes," or if, as others teach, his "thorn in the flesh" was *physical* weakness instead of what Paul himself says it was, "Satan's angel" inflicting the many buffetings which Paul enumerates, how could he labor more abundantly than all the other apostles? Or since he had strength to do more work than all the others, how could his "weaknesses" be *physical?* Since Paul's "thorn" did not hinder his faith for the universal healing of "all the rest of the sick folk on the Island" of Melita, (Moffatt's trans.) why should it hinder *ours?* Would not *Paul's* failure to be healed, if he was sick, hinder the universal faith of these heathen for their healing? Why do traditional teachers substitute "ophthalmia of the eyes" or sickness, (neither of which Paul mentions) for the "reproaches," "necessities," "persecutions," "distresses" and all the other buffetings at the hands of "Satan's angels" which he *does* mention. If the former constitute his "thorn" why does he not say he takes pleasure in the former instead of the latter? How could Paul, sick in body, or with the unsightly disease of "ophthalmia of the eyes," and unable to be healed, "make the Gentiles obedient by word and deed *through mighty signs and wonders?*" (Rom. 15:18-19).

29. If sickness is the will of God, then would not every physician be a law-breaker, every trained nurse be defying the Almighty, every hospital a house of rebellion instead of a house of mercy, and instead of supporting hospitals should we not then do our utmost to close them?

30. Since Jesus in the Gospels never commissioned anybody to preach the Gospel without commanding them to heal the sick, how can we obey this command if there is no Gospel (good news) of healing to proclaim to the sick as a basis for their faith? Or, since faith is expecting God to keep His

promise, how can there be faith for healing if God has not promised it? And since the Bible is full of promises of healing are they not all Gospel (good news) to the sick? Since "faith cometh by hearing . . . the Word" how can the sick have faith for healing if there is nothing for them to hear?

31. "Could the loving heart of the Son of God, Who had compassion upon the sick, and healed all who had need of healing, cease to regard the sufferings of His own when He had become exalted at the right hand of the Father?"—*Kenneth Mackenzie.*

16

Testimonies

Miraculous Healing of One Leads Many to Soul Salvation —Physical Blessings Also Follow

The five testimonies combined under this heading call attention to the spiritual and physical blessings that follow constantly the healing of a single individual. The result of the healing of Aeneas was that all Lydda and Saron turned to God. His healing was as important as the salvation of two cities. Through the healing of the lame man at the beautiful gate of the temple, 5000 men were saved. Paul tells us of God's purpose "to make the Gentiles obedient by word and deed through mighty signs and wonders."

The persons healed constantly receive with such physical blessings an infilling of the Spirit and a compassion for others that send them out to seek the salvation of others and to tell them that they, too, can receive from a loving God the healing that they need for their own bodies.

Thrilling testimonies telling of such a "chain of blessings" are continually being received.

Saved and healed of her affliction, Mrs. J. B. Long, of 38 Clifton Park, North Side, Pittsburgh, Pa., sought to fulfill the promise she made to take a message of Divine healing to some sick friends. Prompted by the Holy Spirit, she went to the altar with her own bodily affliction. Anointed by the Rev. E. D. Whiteside and Evangelist Fred Francis Bosworth she arose to be a spiritual blessing to other. How faithfully she is fulfilling her promise is shown in her determination to carry the Gospel with its messages of bodily healing to the sick in soul and body. Souls saved and bodies healed bring blessed assurance of happiness to the benighted and forsaken.

Cracked Knees—Painful to Walk—Now Climb Steps

More than a year ago I was healed of total deafness in my right ear and also cracked knee-caps. The deafness was due to nervous break-down which I had more than ten years ago and it left me deaf for more than five years. On my way to church one night in company with Miss Elizabeth Taylor, I fell and cracked my knees. They caused me great suffering for several years and kept growing worse all the time.

I could scarcely go up and down the steps, but now, praise God, I can run. I live on the hill top and to take the street car, it is necessary to go down a flight of 185 steps. I used to suffer agony in holding on the rail and trying to get down, but bless His dear name, I can now run down and I never go down those steps without lifting my heart to God in true thankfulness for what He has done.

It was during the first Bosworth Campaign in Pittsburgh, that I was healed. I sat in the meeting looking at the wonderful sight of people being saved and healed. I had been saved 38 years before when I was just a little girl. The thought came to me that night how sweet it would be to be able to take a message of Divine healing to some of my sick friends. Just then the thought came to me how can I carry the gospel of healing to any one unless I have a testimony of my own? That decided me.

Without the least hesitation I went to the altar with my own bodily ills and was anointed. Brother F. F. Bosworth and Rev. E. D. Whiteside prayed with me and I was instantly healed. It was complete and during the year following my healing I have never had any return of the trouble. I was saved to serve and I was anxious to be healed that I might serve Him better. As I walked up Ohio street that night to take the car, I suddenly seemed to be in a new world.

I believe at that time God gave me a fresh baptism of His Holy Spirit. This has been the most wonderful year of my life, for God has so sweetly used me in His service. Truly, there is joy in the service of the King. I have had more spiritual blessings follow my healing and Christ has been nearer and dearer to me than ever before.

I find the great secret of this joy comes from testifying to the power of God. The night I was healed I testified to a member of my Church on the car. I knew it would spread. The following week my pastor called me aside, told me what he had heard and asked if it was true. I told him it was true. He could not see it my way at first, but when I gave him Scripture for it (Matt. 8:16-17) the Lord fully convinced him.

The following week our services opened. It was the best revival we ever knew. One evening each week, our pastor spoke on Divine healing. The invitation went out to those seeking salvation or healing. The pastor anointed, while Brother I. E. Hoover and I laid hands on the sick. Many were healed while we prayed with them.

I felt I was just an empty vessel lying at the Master's feet, ready to be filled and used in His service. The next day after my healing, I asked the Lord to send me to some one who needed healing, that I might tell my story. The face of a friend of mine came before me, Mrs. Sadie Robinson, 11 Brightridge street. I went to call and found her in bed, having been ill for many weeks.

The next day Brother I. E. Hoover offered his machine; we took her to the C. & M. A. Tabernacle, Arch street, where she was anointed by Brother Bosworth and healed. It resulted in the salvation of four in her family. God has been wonderfully using her, to His honor and glory. One of her neighbors, Mrs. Bigley, a great sufferer for 30 years, whose testimony follows, had heard of Mrs. Robinson's healing and sent for her and myself. We spent an afternoon with her studying the Bible together. She was very anxious.

I went again in a few days with Mr. Fred Collins, who was healed at the Bosworth meeting, Mr. I. E. Hoover and the Rev. Kreamer, the Baptist minister. We prayed with Mrs. Bigley, anointed her and she was healed.

This was on Saturday. The following Tuesday she was up, perfectly well, had on her shoes, and without a sign of her old trouble. She was beaming with happiness and she has had no return of any of her troubles which had been of 30 years' duration. Her son was also brought to Christ and healed at the Sheraden Tabernacle.

I find that the most important thing in the Christian life is perfect obedience to the will of God. It is very sweet to live in the inner circle. Although it may cut us off from those around us, yet it is sweet to know we have His approval. —Mrs. J. B. Long, 38 Clifton Park, North Side, Pittsburgh, Pa., December 29, 1921.

Mrs. Taylor Confirms Mrs. Long's Testimony

I am well acquainted with Mrs. Long. We both belong to the same church and I was with her the night she fell and cracked her knee-caps. She was laid up for some time. They were also healed and she has no more trouble with them.—Elizabeth Taylor, 22 Overlook street, North Side, Pittsburgh, Pa., December 29, 1921.

Carried by Three—Came Out Alone—Was Almost Dead—Now Healed

Healing of Nervous Break-Down Results in Salvation of Husband and Three Daughters

In the early fall of last year, 1920, I was taken very ill with nervous break-down of body and mind as well as inward trouble. I was kept at home for two weeks under the care of one of our best doctors. One day I would seemingly be better, but the next day would be worse and so on until some kind friends came and took me to their home in the country. There I was free from all city noise and I received the best treatment and all the love and kindness that one could receive. I was there six weeks, but had just the same results, being kept under a quieting tonic most of the time, nights as well as days.

After six weeks, I was brought back, if anything, worse than before. The next day after being brought home the blessed Lord sent one of His faithful servants to me, Mrs. Mary Long, of 38 Clifton Park, North Side. She gave me her testimony and prayed for me. She was all love and kindness. One day she mended some of my son's greasy working clothes, and another day helped the children prepare the meal. I tell this to the glory of God to show what one will do when the Holy Ghost has the right of way with them.

On Monday, November 15, 1920, she and two others, dear Christians, came with a machine and took me to the Tabernacle on Arch street. There Brother Bosworth prayed for me and anointed me and I was healed immediately. Bless God. Jesus did it in answer to prayer. It took three to help me into the Tabernacle, but I walked out without the aid of a human hand, leaning heavily on the arm of Jesus.

Oh, He was and still is so precious to me. The morning of the 15th, that I was taken to the Tabernacle, my husband and family truly believed I could not possibly live the day out. That evening I prepared the evening meal with very little help from the children. My healing has been the means of my husband and three daughters giving their hearts to Christ. They are standing firmly today on the solid rock, Christ Jesus, praise God.

The next morning, the 16th, I took a street car and went to the meeting without a human being with me. Jesus was with me and still is. The day after that, the 17th, I cleaned three rooms completely, singing and praising God all the time. Since that I have been attacked a few times, and each time the dear Lord has sent Sister Long to me and she has prayed for me, and bless God, each time I have been healed. I truly have much to praise God for.

I knew Sister Long before her healing, how she was afflicted, and since she has been delivered. I praise God for the way He is using her to His glory. May He add His blessing to my testimony.

Your sister in the Lord Jesus Christ, Mrs. Sadie Robinson, 11 Brightridge street, North Side, Pittsburgh, Pa., December 31, 1921.

Nervousness Cured—Suffered for Years

Crafton, Pa.—Miss Hazel D. Benz, 20 Cleveland Avenue. I have suffered from nervous affection for five years. It arose from spinal trouble, the doctors said. I had no control over the muscles in my head. My face and mouth were constantly twitching and distorted. My eyes were similarly affected. My head moved about. Specialist after specialist was consulted. None of them were able to help me. They could not determine what caused the trouble. Finally, I heard of the meeting at the Sheraden Tabernacle. I came November 4th. When the invitation was given I went forward, was prayed for and anointed. The twitching and contortions stopped immediately and have not returned.

In a letter written several months later, confirming her testimony, Miss Benz says:

"Since I was healed of my serious nervous trouble four months ago, my mother, sister, brother-in-law and step-father have been saved. I have myself gained eighteen and one-half pounds in weight."

Varicose Veins—Blood Pressure—Limbs Swelled— Trouble Gone

In commemoration of the birth of our Lord and Savior, Jesus Christ on this beautiful Christmas day, I know of no better tribute than the testimony of my dear mother and myself. I hope in giving it, that it may be used to bring peace and joy to some poor tired sinner or to help some poor sufferer to be healed, all "to the Glory of God."

About five months ago, my mother, who had been troubled with varicose veins for over 30 years, an awful high blood pressure and swelling of the limbs developing into a dropsical condition for nearly 10 years, and who had been unable to walk for 10 weeks, heard of one of our neighbors, Mrs. Robinson, being healed by "faith in God." The case was so wonderful that we inquired and found out that a Mrs. J. B. Long had taken this woman to some church; so we found where Mrs. Long lived and asked her to come and see mother. Mrs. Robinson and Mrs. Long came and prayed with mother and explained the wonderful things in store for all who believed. Later, Mrs. Long and three of the church came to see us, prayed with mother and anointed her. Three days later, she could put her shoes on and walk, which she had not done for 10 long weeks.

Meanwhile, mother had read her Bible, and as God revealed Himself to her in prayer, she was greatly blessed and all the pain and aches left her limbs, the varicose veins started to dry up and all swelling receded. Her general health became better and the high blood pressure began to disappear, something that the doctors had claimed was impossible except by electric treatments. They had advised her removal to a hospital months ago.

Today finds mother in better health than she has been in years and there has been no return of any of her old ailments. Glory to God for His blessings. Being saved and healed herself, she has found consolation and happiness in the work of God and in His promises.

Meanwhile Mrs. Long continued to call on us. She was never in a hurry to go and always had prayer before leaving.

When I saw the wonderful works of God in my mother, I too, started to search the Scriptures and found God's promises were the same to me if I believed. On one of Mrs. Long's visits, she told me of her own life and of others. After telling me it was the last day of the Tabernacle services, she persuaded me to go. Well, with Mrs. Robinson and her husband, who had also been saved and healed, I went. It was a day I will never forget as long as I live.

After listening to the evangelist, at the end of his sermon, he called for all who wished to be saved or healed or prayed for to come forward. All the time I had been listening, I had been silently praying for God to lead me. With Brother Robinson, I went forward and I was saved by the blood of Christ.

I had been suffering from nervous disorders and bad health for 15 years, had been through three very serious operations and never had a well day. After being prayed for and anointed by one of the workers, I came home and glory to God, "by His stripes" I was healed. I have enjoyed my meals ever since, have never been bothered with any stomach trouble at all and my nerves have been strengthened wonderfully. Mother and I are so happy and the further on we go the sweeter this life gets. It seems we both are getting the good things God has in store for all who believe. I also want to mention this: in one week I prayed to God for five things which a person would think were nearly impossible, but glory be to His holy name, I got all I asked for.

Please print this so that some one may see it and profit by our experience and get peace and happiness like we did. All who believe on the Lord Jesus Christ shall be saved. This is His promise and praise His blessed name He never breaks His promises. Our Bible is a great source of happiness now and my one hope is that God may use me in the advancement of His work in any way He chooses. We are thankful to God and will always be His co-workers here until He takes us to be wtih Him over there.—Carson A. Bigley, 1321 Pennsylvania avenue, North Side, Pittsburgh, Pa., December 25, 1917.

Eye Specialists Outrivaled by Simple Faith

I was a church member and had been one for five years. I knew that Jesus was the Son of God and that He shed his blood on the cross. But I did not know—had never heard that it was for me—that I was lost and that I could be saved and know it—instead of waiting until I died to learn whether I got to heaven or not.

However, I was proud of the church and would never think of going into another denomination's meeting. But I was in need of healing. I had been very far-sighted all my life and had been cross-eyed in one eye for fifteen years. I wore powerful glasses for over eleven years and had to have them changed by a specialist about every six months. When deprived of my glasses for just a few moments, I would suffer severe headaches, and could not see well enough to distinguish faces or furniture. Everything would be hazy and blurred.

A friend, in Pittsburgh, sent me a *Tribune* giving testimonies and announcing the Bosworth meetings in Detroit. I went to the meeting January 11, 1921, and was saved right in my seat. I don't remember the text or anything about that night except that I felt much lighter when I went out than when I came in. That week the Lord began dealing with me, and "behold old things passed away and all things became as new."

The next morning, I went up for healing. Brother B. B. Bosworth prayed for me and I was instantly healed. He held up the seeker's card and I could read everything on it. I was just dumfounded. For two hours my eyes were perfectly straight and my vision normal. Then both went back and were worse than they had ever been all the rest of that day and all the next day.

Some of the folks at home tried to urge me to put my glasses back on—they said that I would go blind altogether. But, thank God—I refused and just trusted Him. The following day my eyes were perfectly straight and kept getting stronger all along, until now they are just as normal as anyone's. I forgot to mention that during the time the Lord was testing me, I could read my Bible, but nothing else. Two weeks after the Lord so wonderfully healed me, He baptized and filled me with the Holy Ghost and still keeps me filled.

I do praise God that He put healing in the Gospel and that the Bosworth Brothers ever came to Detroit and told us about it. Since the Lord healed me, I have never had the headache from my eyes.

There is no one more real to me than my Lord and He is nearer and dearer each day. I could never begin to tell what He has done for me. Almost every time I give my testimony, I hear of some one who has been helped either physically or spiritually.

I praise God that He cares for all things that concern us. When the Lord told us to go to St. Paul, we had only two cents (Mrs. Monroe and I). After we told the Lord we would go, He gave us the fare. I had never heard of any such thing as trusting the Lord for financial aid, 'till Mr. Bosworth told of his experiences. "Faith cometh by hearing, and hearing by the Word of God."

One morning, we had thirteen cents; after getting a light breakfast, we had one cent left. So we cried out, shouting "Glory" in the pocketbooks. (No one knew that we had gone on faith). At the exact time that we did this, a special delivery letter was sent to us with two dollars in it. Three days later, when our rent was due, the Lord sent in fourteen dollars. That is the way He provided. When I was coming home, we had five dollars and twelve cents. I asked the Lord for my fare. By twelve that night (Saturday), He sent it in and one dollar and eighty-five cents more.

I have had to rely on His promises for everything since, and He has never failed me.

Use this testimony as you see fit—by the guidance of the Holy Spirit and all for the glory of God.

Mrs. Edith I. Watt Lau, 3704 Wabash Avenue, Detroit, Mich.

(This testimony was given a year after her healing.)

Healed of Cancer

About four years ago, a cancer started on my face. It was, at first, apparently only a small wart on my nose. I kept scratching it until it became a sore, and then it was apparent that a cancer had developed. At that time I suffered very much, but before the second year the pain and agony were extreme.

It was necessary to keep my face covered, both on account of its appearance and the necessity of keeping cloths saturated with ether and other anaesthetics to check the pain. I spent about $500.00 for anaesthetics during the last year I was sick. This was the only means of easing the suffering. When I removed the cloth, the pain was so intense that I was blinded and could not see my hand before my face.

I went from one physician to another in Ohio, Indiana, New York and New Jersey, wherever I heard of a good one, looking for relief. I am sure I consulted more than fifty of them. But all of them said there was no hope and that they could do nothing for me.

But praise the Lord, in September, 1920, I heard of the Bosworth meetings which were being held in my home town, Lima, Ohio. I went prompted by no other desire than to get healed. I had never heard the gospel preached in this way before and went forward immediately. When I was asked to pray I did not know how and the words had to be put in my mouth, but as I repeated them, faith came into my heart, and I began to be very happy.

They laid hands on me for healing and as they did so I could feel the power of God going through my body. It rose up into my face. The feeling was that of a tight rubber cap over my face which was being slipped off, little by little. When it reached the top of my head, I saw a bright light and I had a vision of Jesus standing right before me. Then I shouted in earnest, although I had not been able to do so before. As soon as the hands were laid on me, the pain ceased, and I knew I was healed. Others tell me I cried out, "I am saved and healed," and that I threw away the cloth which had covered my face. I was so happy that I was not aware of what I was doing. I shouted and shouted with joy, went home shouting, shouting almost all night and continued shouting when I arose in the morning.

When I arose, my daughter had gotten breakfast. She looked at me and exclaimed, "Oh, mother!" There was a big looking glass in the dining room and I looked in that. I saw that my upper lip, parts of which had been eaten away previously, was healed. It had been eaten away so that the roots of my teeth showed. During the night it had filled in with new flesh, was covered with fresh skin and was as solid and clear as it is at present. There were no traces left of the cancer except the scars. Two scabs which had been on my face were still there, but later disappeared. But wherever the skin had been gone it was completely healed during the night and the new skin had formed.

My right thumb had been crippled for four years. My instep had been broken. They were both healed at the same time as the cancer. I have not had pain from either of them since that time.

When I saw that my lip was restored, I shouted so loud that the home soon filled up with neighbors, to whom I told the story of what God had done for me.

My children took my healing as an indication that the Lord would soon take me to heaven and if I went out to the neighbors and stayed longer than I expected they would come to see if I was still on the earth.

For two years I had not been able to take anything except soup or milk. I could not open my mouth far enough to take food in, and had to sip liquid from a small spoon held to my lips. I was healed on Friday night, and on Saturday morning I took up knife and fork and began to eat just as I did before I was afflicted. When the Bosworth

Brothers came to see me the same morning, I took a large tablespoon, opened my mouth wide and showed them how I could eat then. When they came, I was out visiting the neighbors and showing them my face, but they waited at my home until I returned and rejoiced with me over the healing.

On Sunday, I went out to be baptized. On Saturday, something had said to me, "go into the water." Brother Bosworth explained to me what it meant and I obeyed and was baptized.

On Monday, my daughter had a bushel of apples and I sat peeling them and singing, "I know the Lord laid His hands on me; He healed the sick and raised the dead." I peeled the whole bushel before I realized that something had happened to my crippled hand. Then I found it was perfectly well.

As soon as the news of my healing spread, I had many callers asking for confirmation of it. I received letters from all over the world asking about it and one day I received nineteen. I also had many out-of-town callers on the same errand. I was able to refer them to any of my neighbors about my previous condition, as all knew it.

Three months ago, a doctor who had formerly prescribed for me, came to my house. He asked me how I was getting along. I told him I was well and praising the Lord. He wanted to know what doctor I had. I told him, "Dr. Jesus." He said, "How long has he been here?" I answered, "As long as I have." He did not know that I meant the Lord Jesus Christ. When he understood he shouted with laughter and was very happy over it.

On Monday, after peeling the apples, I went and prayed for a woman who had a cancer. She went to the meeting a night or two afterward and was healed. As I came out of her house praising the Lord, I passed the gas plant. The men working there asked me what the matter was. One of them must have been a Christian for when I told them, he began to shout.

Since my healing a year ago, I have not had any symptoms whatever of the cancer or any pain in my hand or foot, but about a month before coming to Toledo, I let a very large lump of coal fall on my foot. It was very badly bruised. Three or four days before I came here, a piece of bone about one-half inch long, came out of it. After coming to Toledo, I was prayed for and the foot healed. There has been no pain in it since then.

Since I was saved, I have been called away many times to pray for the sick. In one case, it was a little boy, Billy Jones, who had been confined to his bed for several months. He was paralyzed and had bad sores on his back and face. I prayed for him and told the parents that in nine days he would walk. I said that, because it seemed that a voice came to me with that message. In just nine days from that time, he walked to my house, two blocks away.

One day last winter, I was without coal. I knew that the Lord had promised to take care of me, so I prayed about it. On going down stairs I found a lump of coal that filled a bushel basket when we broke it up. I never learned who sent it. When I pray for anything I need, I am sure to get it, just as if I had a friendly neighbor and she had given it to me. I do not always get it right away, but it comes nevertheless.

Just before I came to Toledo on this visit, I said to the Lord, "I would like to be in the Bosworth meetings once more." He immediately provided the money for me to go to Toledo. I knew I was going to a strange place, so I said, "Lord, I know you are going to take care of me." Through no effort of mine, He provided a beautiful place for me to stay while here.

When I had the cancer, I was obliged to sell my clothes to provide money for the ether, drugs and other needs; so when I was healed, I was necessarily poor. But He has provided ever since. I have never wanted for a thing.

The first of April, last, we were exposed to the smallpox. The authorities quarantined us and would not provide for us. I prayed and one day when we had run out of everything, there stood a man at the door with a great big basket of things. Both my daughter and I had a bad case of the disease but had no physician except Jesus and came out all right, without any scars.

After nearly three years of suffering, to be instantly set free! It is almost too good to be true.

Miss Lida Clark's Confirmation of Mrs. Alice Baker's Cancer Testimony

I was present at the time Mrs. Baker was healed of her cancer. After she had been anointed and prayed for, she said to some one, "Take that cloth off." The other person loosened it from her face and Mrs. Baker took it and threw it away. She appeared to be just filled with the Holy Spirit. She cried out, "I am saved and healed," as she sprang to her feet. It could not have appeared to the audience that she was healed, any more than it did to me. Her face was a horrible sight. It was a mass of blood, pus and open sores. But she said afterwards that the pain had ceased and that she had the assurance in her heart that she was healed.

The odor from the cancer was so offensive that the worker who filled out her card, was sick from it that evening and all the next day. But there was no odor the next night. I sat right alongside of her and know that this was the case.

And the cancer, the holes in her lip and all the sores had disappeared. She was healed—that was undeniable.

After her healing, I saw a physician who had treated her during her illness. After hearing that she had been healed, he asked me to tell him what I had actually seen. I told him that I saw her come in with the cloth on her face, was present when she was prayed for, heard her say, as she took the cloth off, that she was healed, and saw her walk down the street without the cloth.

He said that it was impossible, that she could not walk out without the cloth over her face, because the pain would have been so intense as to blind her and she could not find her way out of the hall. He said, "Girl, you have been hypnotized, that could not be so."

I saw him again after he had seen her, and he said it certainly was a marvelous thing for her. He acknowledged it was so.

Miss Lida Clark, 682½ S. Main St., Lima, Ohio.

Monster Cancer Healed

Chicago, Ill., Mrs. R. Jerolaman of 7111 Eberhart avenue. —I visited Mrs. Trina Odegard, 224 Hoy avenue, Woodstock, Ill., May, 1921, and was greatly surprised to see her in the condition in which I found her, more dead than alive. We knew she had suffered with ulcers of the stomach for twenty-five years or more and were of the opinion she had a cancer. Her meal consisted of a half slice of bread, and when I urged her to eat more, she told me if she did, the pains would kill her. She was barely able to walk across the floor.

After I left, she consulted three physicians in Woodstock; had an X-ray photograph taken and learned she had a

serious case of cancer, far too advanced to even suggest an
operation, as the physicians gave as their opinion she would
never pull through. They gave her about two weeks to
live. She decided to consult a specialist here in Chicago, and
he told her the same thing. It was during this visit in July,
1921, that she heard of the Bosworth tent meetings at Cicero
and North Avenues. She was taken there at once and when
prayed for, was healed instantly. She said the power of God
went down through her body from head to foot during the
prayer.

Her soreness, pain and suffering were all over instantly.
The cancer was eliminated by the power of God. She was
so hungry before leaving the tent, she could hardly wait
until she got where she could get something to eat. She
visited us the next day, ate the heartiest meal I had ever
seen her eat in many a year and there was not the slightest
evidence of serious after-effect.

It has been six months since her healing, and when I
called her up the other evening, she was getting along fine.
She has gained in weight and is hungry all the time. The
people in Woodstock were astonished, as they never expected to see her return alive, after making the trip to
Chicago.

It was through her wonderful healing that mother and I
were saved. We wanted to serve a God that was so loving
and we gave our hearts to Him right then and there. I
am happier every day since I was converted.

These, however, are not all the blessings we received. I
had been ailing and doctoring for almost four years. I was
so nervous that at times I almost went into hysterics. I was
terribly anemic and also had internal trouble for which I
had undergone an operation two and a half years before.
After that, I was worse than ever, not being able to gain

weight or strength, whatever I did. I took nerve tonic, blood tonics and serum injections. Nothing seemed to do me any good. I became disgusted with life and decided to stop doctoring.

I thank God that He led me to the Bosworth tent meetings, as I know He wanted me to go there so that He might save and heal me. I was not saved before that and my healing came as soon as I gave myself to Jesus. I am gaining in weight, am stronger than I have ever been and am not nervous any more. I also thank God for the perfect peace and joy that I have in my heart, and life with Christ is all joy and happiness.

Mother experienced a wonderful healing. One doctor said I had better see that she was taken care of immediately or I would not have her with me very long. He said that she must have an operation for gall and appendix trouble as the pains were so severe she could not sleep. She had undergone an operation seven years ago and had not been well since. She also suffered an abdominal rupture after returning home from the hospital and so dreaded the thought of another operation. After being prayed for, she felt the power of God going through her and cried for joy. Her pains have left her entirely, and, praise the Lord, the rupture is being healed.

Mrs. Killick's Testimony

I had suffered for years with a cancer on the leg. The pain caused me to tear my hair and was too intense to describe. The doctors operated but brought no relief. For two years after the operation I had not been able to lace my boot on account of the swelling, nor could I walk properly, kneel down, do my work or go out. The cancer was pronounced a Melanotic Sarcoma. I had been confined to my bed continuously for four months.

Soon after being anointed and prayed with, the pain almost instantaneously left, and the swelling rapidly disappeared. The cancer has now completely gone and only a few scars show where the black monster with its hideous head lived. The flesh has become pure and clean and my health is perfect.

After being healed, I went to the doctor, who simply laughed and said, "Well, I am pleased to see it, Mrs. Killick, but I will bet you ten dollars it will be back in six months."

It is now nearly two years and my condition is as described.

Mrs. Killick, 45 Ferrier street, Toronto.

Healing of Miss Nix

In October, 1921, I was healed by the power of God from cancer, sugar diabetes and enlargement of the heart, a twisted spine, almost total paralysis from the hips to the feet, the condition of being a nervous wreck and of almost total blindness. I had suffered from the cancer for one and a half years, and from the other troubles for seven years. I walked only with crutches and when I went out, it was in a wheel chair. The doctor who treated me said, a few weeks ago, that I had been one of the greatest sufferers he had known.

About the twelfth of October, I had a bad spell and sent for the doctor. He said that I had about ten days to live, and no more. On October the fifteenth, a little man who was in the habit of bringing my newspaper, came to the door and inquired as to my condition. He asked to see me and was granted permission with the suggestion that I undoubtedly would not recognize him. Before he went out I knew him but was unable to speak.

He said, "Mrs. Killick, who has been healed of a terrible cancer is coming here. Would you like to see her?" I

nodded assent. She came to see me and told me that God
wanted to heal me. She read the Bible to me and prayed,
but I do not remember now what she said. She sang a hymn
and I do remember that. It was:

> *Were the whole realm of nature mine,*
> *That were a present far too small.*
> *Love, so amazing, so Divine,*
> *Demands my soul, my life, my all.*

She departed saying that she would come back again
at night. I lay in bed thinking, and when my friend who
was taking care of me came in, I said, "If God has healed
that woman He will heal me."

I asked the Lord what He would have me do and I heard
Him say plainly, "Put on your shoes and stockings." My
friends said, "Dear, you cannot get up," but she brought
the shoes and stockings. She lifted my foot to dress it and I
felt no difference, but the moment the stocking touched my
foot, I felt the power of God touch my body. It started at
my feet just where I was obeying the command, and spread
all over my body. I got up on my feet, although I had not
stood alone for four years. Then I asked to have my clothes
brought to me and I dressed alone. I walked into the bed-
room and did up my hair. My friend asked, "What are
you going to do now?" I said that I was going to help her
get supper. She asked me what I was going to eat, and I
told her the same as she was. Previously, I had eaten only
eggs and orange juice. I ate just what she ate.

I went to bed at nine and slept until six in the morning.
I could not stay abed, but got up, ate breakfast, washed the
dishes and asked God what He would like to have me do to
glorify Him. I heard Him say, "Wax the floor." The tempter
said, "You cannot do that, you have not been on your knees
for years." I waxed the floor from end to end, and Mrs.

234 *Christ the Healer*

Killick saw it completed when she returned in the afternoon. She said, "I am going to give my testimony in the little Salvation Army Hall. Will you give yours?"

She offered to get an automobile to take me down, but I refused and walked all the way. When I reached there, the power of God so overcame me, I could not speak and remained but a few moments.

From that hour to this God has given me strength and guided my steps. Last summer, I had charge of one of the largest summer homes of the Anglican Church, and often worked from six in the morning until two or three o'clock the next morning. I have been feeling perfectly well ever since my healing except for an attack of pneumonia from which the Lord delivered me without the aid of medicine or physician. *My testimony has been a means of blessing to many, and some of the girls attending our own little Mission Hall which I was led to open in faith, have been converted and healed through it.*

Do you wonder that I love God? He has blessed me spiritually as well as physically and I am sure I am the happiest woman on earth. *Better than my own healing He has used me mightily to tell others what He has done for me, and many have been wonderfully healed.*

Miss R. Nix, 412 Dundas street, E., Toronto.

Miraculous Healing Followed by Conversion of Twenty Relatives

I have been suffering with stomach trouble for many years (about 30 years). Twenty years ago I had the first operation for tumor. I got to the place where nothing stayed on my stomach and could not think of eating fruit. I have had three operations since the first one. Had fourteen different doctors attending me. Got to the place where I could not

even take any more medicine on account of the condition
of my stomach. Found I had a fallen stomach. Last June
I found I had an inward goiter. My condition grew worse.
At last I found I had cancer. I went to the People's Tabernacle at Bethlehem, Pa., and was anointed and prayed for
and God did so compassionately touch my body, praise His
Name! I cried for joy. The Lord has never been so dear to
me. I did not realize He loved me so. Things are different.
I see that He was just waiting to come and heal me. I am
healed of all my diseases, praise His name!

What is still better, I brought my husband, mother, daughter, sons, sisters, and brothers, sister-in-law, nieces and one
nephew. Twenty in all, and they were all converted. God
made a clean sweep. "Thou shalt be saved and thy house."—
Mrs. Edward A. Bander, F.R.D. No. 3, Easton, Pa.

Healed of Bright's Disease and Other Ailments

While listening to the full Gospel, which I heard you
preach in St. Petersburg, Fla., last January, I received untold
spiritual and physical blessings; and it was such a revelation
to me to know that God is so willing to heal, that I hope and
pray I may be used to tell others.

After doctoring for five years for Bright's disease, high
blood pressure (240 and over), sinus infection, and several
minor ailments, I was told that I could live only three
months.

I had been to numerous doctors of high reputation in the
United States and Canada, (Mayo Bros. and John Hopkins),
to chiropractors and osteopaths, and felt that everything had
been done that human aid could do.

But, thank God, He wonderfully healed me physically,
and I feel like a new person. Spells that I used to have three
times a week have not returned since. My blood pressure

is down and the doctor told me that my heart was normal.
And I was able to immediately discard my glasses, which I
have had to wear for years.—Lela Beach, Cornwall, Ont.,
Canada.

Nurse Healed of Varicose Veins

For the past four years I have suffered with varicose veins.
It was impossible for me to stand on my feet even for a few
minutes without constantly shifting my weight from one foot
to the other. Three different times for four months at a
time, I was compelled to stay off my feet entirely.

My limbs were so badly swollen and inflamed that I could
not bear any covering over them, even in the winter time,
and I always slept with the windows open and my limbs
exposed to the cold air regardless of the temperature of the
room.

Several days ago I came to the tabernacle, and, after receiving instruction and teaching on divine healing, I was
anointed and prayed for. I am entirely free from pain in
my body, and am able to work every day without any dis-
comfort. The knots or lumps on my limbs were the size of
hen's eggs, but they have completely disappeared; praise the
Lord!

I wish to thank God also, for the healing of my little ten-
year-old daughter. She had suffered with chronic bronchitis
all her life, continually under the doctor's care and yet never
free from coughing day and night. Since being anointed
and prayed for, she has been entirely delivered, for which
we praise His dear name.

I shall be glad to have this testimony published for His
glory and the blessing of others.—Beth P. Evans, No. 2
Ackley Ave., Johnson City, N. Y.

Lord Couldn't Wait! Eager to Bless His Children

In 1914, some time in December, I was unloading cars of coal and in some way I twisted my back. I started for my home, but was picked up and carried home, as I could not walk because of the intense suffering.

For three months I could not walk, and for three years I could not sleep on a bed. I had to sleep on the floor, as I could not bear to lie on anything that was not perfectly flat. My left side was paralyzed, and was so numb I could hardly walk.

When I heard of the Bosworth brothers coming here, and read of their great faith in the Lord for healing, I felt my time had come to be healed. I got a healing card, but when I came forward and found that I could not be prayed for until the card had been numbered, I just felt like that man of whom we read in the Bible, who every time he came to the pool at the troubling of the waters, was always too late, and someone else had slipped in ahead of him.

I was standing in front of the platform, feeling very much disappointed, and as I turned to go back to my seat the Lord spoke to me and said: "If you are willing, I will make you whole!" I said, "Lord, I am willing." Praise the Lord, He straightened my back and healed the paralyzed side, and I can go to bed now and sleep like a baby.

Praise the Lord, and may He heal all that come to Him, is my prayer.--Harvey B. Whitecotton, 1502 Bates St., Indianapolis, Ind.

Crippled and Deformed from Infantile Paralysis; Instantly Healed

I want you to tell everybody and read this in your meetings, so everyone will know what God has done for me.

When I was one year old I had Infantile Paralysis. Had to walk on my toe and my heel was up to the top of my shoe. My foot also turned outward. Last Wednesday, February 17th, our kind neighbor, Mrs. Howell, called to me and asked me to go with her to the Bosworth meetings, saying that I would be healed if I were a good boy and did no bad deeds. I asked Auntie, who is very old and who is keeping our home together for father since my mother died with the "Flu," and she said I might go. I came with Mrs. Howell for three evenings. On Friday, February 19th, I was anointed and prayed for. We had only reached our seat a few minutes when my heel went down and my foot went over to the other one. It felt just as if someone took hold and pulled it down and then over to the other one. Now I can step on my whole foot and put my feet together like any of my other brothers. Today, three days after being healed, I'm learning to use roller skates. I'm the happiest boy in Easton. I am thirteen years old. I want you to tell other crippled boys what God has done for me. I will always thank Him and pray every day and ask Him to help other little boys.—John Jr. Snyder, 600 S. 23rd St., Easton, Pa.

Woman Dumb Is Instantly Healed

More than three years ago through sickness, I completely lost my power of speech. I have had several physicians and all told me I could never regain my voice. Some of them told me that the vocal organs were paralyzed. During all this time I have never been able to make an audible sound.

I have also been a great sufferer from Rheumatism and Gall-stones. My friends tried to make me think it would do me no good to go to Bethlehem to be anointed for healing, but I came and was anointed and prayed for on February 2nd and was instantly healed. When I walked from the platform back to my seat I found my voice completely restored so that after three years of total silence I could speak normally and can ever since, praise the Lord! My pastor, who did not believe I could be healed, was greatly surprised to find I could talk when I met him on the street. He said, "I have been a 'doubting Thomas,' but now I am compelled to believe."

The pastor of the Baptist Church in Bangor asked me to come to his church on Sunday, which I did. After telling the audience about the miracle, he had me stand and show them how I could speak.

I was also healed of my Rheumatism and Gall-stones. I am so thankful to God for His mercy.—Mrs. Thomas Hughes, 151 Northhampton St., Bangor, Pa.

Woman Instantly Healed of Two Cancers
Answer to Prayer

Fifteen years ago my health broke and I was compelled to give up my work, as my whole body seemed to be filled with some kind of poison that puzzled the doctors. For twelve years I suffered untold agony without any hope of ever being well again. Three and a half years ago I grew so much worse that I had a doctor four months steady, and got worse all the time. Was later told I had a cancer at the mouth of the large bowel and fastened to the spleen. I grew worse and the poison affected my left arm and side until I was drawn crooked and would scream with agony and pain and beg the folks to hold my arm tight as it felt as though it were being pulled out of the socket. Later the cancer spread to my mouth, going in from the throat and under the tongue until it was as thick as another tongue and the roots spread out and wrapped the membrane under my tongue. A Philadelphia physician, after treating me for a while, urged me to. go to the Philadelphia Hospital to see if they would use radium. After several of the professors there examined me, they decided they could do nothing for me, as the cancer in my side was fastened to the spleen and the one in my mouth was fast to a blood artery, so I came home to die. I was a hopeless case. They could do nothing. I started to pray to God to have mercy, and wept in my room alone, and talked with Almighty God in Jesus' name until He took all fear from me. I made up my mind to suffer until He called me. I got to the place where I was taking eighteen doses of medicine a day; nine doses of asafoetida to hold my nerves and stomach and to keep me from vomiting, as I had violent headaches and turns of vomiting. Suffered this way for two years, but thank God for Christian friends who persuaded me to go to the Bosworth meetings being held in Philadelphia. I prayed about it until the Lord showed me to go. I thank God I obeyed. I heard the Gospel in mighty power preached there. I went to the enquiry room three times and heard the instructions. I then got the Evangelist's book "Christ the Healer," studied the references and found that healing was for me. On Monday night, June 14, I went to the platform and was anointed for healing, and, praise God, He met me right there and I was instantly healed. When I was being prayed for I felt a shock go through my body just like electricity. It seemed as though someone grasped the cancer under my tongue and was drawing it out of my mouth. I was instantly healed then and there of my terrible cancers, have taken no medicine since that time, am eating whatever I want and have no pain whatever. I thank God that the Bosworth Party ever came to Philadelphia. May God bless them every one. I hope this will help some other sufferer to the glorious deliverance I have found. —Mrs. B. Edwards, 4120 Westfield Ave., Camden, N. J.

Possibly not one out of ten of those who have been healed have sent us their testimony, yet thousands of testimonies have been received from those healed since those published in this chapter were received. During the past few years thousands of our radio listeners whom we have never seen, after reading our healing literature have written to us asking us to pray for their healing. We have presented these requests in prayer to God, one at a time, and we are still receiving a continuous stream of wonderful testimonies from those healed of every affliction we know anything about. Many have been healed through their own faith which came to them while reading former editions of this book. As high as 72 deaf and dumb from birth after reading this book have been healed when prayed for during a single revival. Again we say, to God be all the glory.

Dear reader, why not have an extra copy of this book to loan to your sick friends? You can thus save them from premature death to a life of service for God. What has been accomplished in this way is a wonderful story.

The Ideal Gift for Those Who Count

SPECIAL OFFER

$5.00

or

2 for $9.00

or

3 for $12.00

GOD SO LOVED THE WORLD
BOB BOSWORTH . . . and the sound of MISSIONS

Is it possible for a Christian to mechanically project, through means of music, the eternal love of God for a not-so-pretty world? This was the question that inspired this album. Bob Bosworth had often shared with audiences in churches, missionary conventions, and elsewhere, the burden and compassion God had placed in his heart for a world that desperately needed the love that only God could give. Through songs that were close to Bob's heart, the Holy Spirit had often electrified a meeting with God's unseen presence. Many Christians reluctantly leaving these meetings, often wished it were possible to recapture the anointing of the services they had attended. With this in mind, Bob prayed for God's anointing as he recorded, and we feel that this has been accomplished. This album was not intended for entertainment, but for effect. If you will commit yourself to the Lord in prayer each time before playing it, you will know His presence and He will speak to your heart. This is THE SOUND OF MISSIONS.

JUST RELEASED!!
TWO NEW RECORDS BY BOB BOSWORTH

THE GLORY OF HIS PRESENCE
An album of new and old songs reflecting the Christian's experience in his quest for God's Will.

RIVERS OF LIVING WATER
A collection of solos and duets, a musical expression by Bob and Stella Bosworth of the Spiritual Life that flows from God's Throne—includes the "click" song from South Africa.

Order From: R. V. BOSWORTH • BOX 4402 • DALLAS, TEXAS 75208
The proceeds from the sale of this record will go toward the support of world missions.